EUROPE AND AMERICA—
THE NEXT TEN YEARS

EUROPE AND AMERICA—

THE NEXT TEN YEARS

by W. Randolph Burgess and
James Robert Huntley

With an Introduction by Livingston T. Merchant

 **WALKER AND COMPANY · NEW YORK**

First published in the United States of America
in 1970 by the Walker Publishing Company, Inc.
Published simultaneously in Canada
by The Ryerson Press, Toronto.
ISBN: 0-8027-0324-0
Library of Congress Catalog Card Number: 70-126108
PRINTED IN THE UNITED STATES OF AMERICA.

Designed by Paula Wiener

CONTENTS

To many friends, young and old,
who have helped to shape this book.

EUROPE AND AMERICA—
THE NEXT TEN YEARS

INTRODUCTION

During the 1960's, a number of books were published here and abroad on various aspects of European-American relations. Many, notably the ten volumes written in connection with the Council on Foreign Relations' five-year study of the Atlantic Community, yielded valuable insights.

About a year ago, George Franklin, who is both Executive Director of the Council on Foreign Relations and Secretary of the Atlantic Council of the United States, suggested that the Atlantic Council consider supplementing the available studies with a single volume attempting to look forward through the 1970's, describe what kind of Atlantic Community would be most advantageous for its peoples, and suggest how fresh progress in that direction might best be made. This book is the result.

A small committee was formed to undertake this examination. Its members were Theodore C. Achilles, George V. Allen, Gene Bradley, W. Randolph Burgess, Jay Cerf, William Diebold, Jr., Isaiah Frank, George S. Franklin, Jr., Theodore Geiger, Lincoln Gordon, H. Field Haviland, Jr., J. Warren Nystrom, Cortlandt V. R. Schuyler, Gerard C. Smith, Robert Triffin, Richard J. Wallace, Francis O. Wilcox, Burke Wilkinson and myself. Collectively, the group represented years of experience in Atlantic affairs, through the channels of diplomacy, politics, academia, journalism, business, and the military.

3

The study group concluded that a searching new approach was needed. Neither a history of the past nor a simple reading of the crystal ball would suffice. Rather it was felt that the work should examine the foreseeable needs of the Atlantic Community—economic, social, military, and political—the most important current trends, the forces of change, and the resultant challenges and opportunities which will have to be faced in the coming decade.

As a basis for this undertaking, the Council and its Paris associate, the Atlantic Institute, had fortunately completed a number of related studies, and there were also available the results of a series of conferences which had brought together leaders in business, academic life, and public affairs from both sides of the Atlantic.

To assemble and analyze the material and produce a basic draft, the Council retained James R. Huntley, a former Foreign Service Officer who subsequently had served as the Executive Secretary of the Atlantic Institute and later as a Ford Foundation executive. W. Randolph Burgess, a Vice Chairman of the Council, former Under Secretary of the Treasury and subsequently U. S. Ambassador to NATO, joined in the project as co-author.

Incorporated in the book are many suggestions and contributions from the members of the Committee, with whom the authors consulted. While neither this Committee nor the Board of the Atlantic Council of the United States is responsible for all the views expressed in this volume, we feel that the authors have brought to their task a rare combination of experience and constructive outlook which has enabled them to produce a book that should help chart the future course of the Atlantic Community.

SOME GENERAL OBSERVATIONS

Before plunging the reader into the detailed chapters of this book, which deal with the different aspects of the subject, a few general observations seem to me appropriate.

The first point, never to be forgotten, is that the greatest achievement in the Atlantic area in the past twenty years has been that the North Atlantic Treaty—together with NATO, the organization created to execute the purposes of the Treaty—has kept the peace in Europe. The policy of deterrence which it has so far successfully followed has provided a shield of security behind which NATO's members were enabled to recover from the physical and spiritual ravages of World War II.

It should also be re-emphasized that the North Atlantic Treaty, and operations under it, are in full accord with both the letter and the spirit of the United Nations. In fact NATO has given powerful reinforcement to the UN's peace-keeping efforts.

The continuing need for NATO to preserve the peace remains clear to all who will look at the continuing evidence of the Soviet Union's growing armaments, its constantly reiterated long-term political intentions, the combination of its determination to control its satellites—witness Czechoslovakia—and its readiness to intrude its political influence and its military presence into areas which it finds tempting by reason of weakened influence or withdrawal on the part of countries friendly to us—witness today the Middle East and the Mediterranean.

The need for the NATO deterrent remains in order to continue to keep the peace. And the need for assurance that the peace will be kept is of crucial importance to that group of countries which is loosely called the Atlantic community. This is because its members need to adapt their economies and many of their institutions to the revolutionary onrush of science and technology which is engulfing us all. And in order to adapt ourselves to these changes we must be free from the fear of external interference or intrusion.

Behind the shield of NATO, confidence returned to Europe and plans for political and economic unity developed. Only a few years ago the so-called Grand Design was widely accepted as a pattern for future European-American relations, arousing enthusiasm on both sides of the ocean. Under this concept a United Europe would become an equal partner with America in great cooperative achievements in defense, trade, and culture.

Then the impetus of the design was lost. The European community was stalled in its tracks and seemed incapable of enlarging itself to become really Europe or of achieving anything more inspiring than a customs union—and a pretty selfish one at that. The intransigence of General de Gaulle in office combined with powerful but short-sighted political, economic, and agricultural interests to block progress. Thus a great postwar surge towards unity in ideas and in actions ground almost to a standstill, marked by a worrisome inflation and widespread revolts in the ranks of students and labor.

From the point of view of long-range political policy, this has been a calamity, for the Grand Design was the focus of attention and planning, a great stimulus to forward progress. It formed the theme of hopeful, concluding chapters of book after book. With this hope blunted, the great countries of the Atlantic area now badly need to reformulate their aims and to recapture the enthusiasm of the partnership—or find some new source of inspiration.

Fresh thought and new approaches are needed to provide Atlantic relationships suited to our times, with appeal to the idealism of the new generation.

The Winds Blow Hard and Change Comes Fast

The speed and significance of change today is hard to comprehend, and this is part of our trouble. Customs, habits of thought, and institutions, whether of government or of learning, are falling behind. Worldwide and society-wide unrest—among poor and rich, ignorant and educated, all races, all nations and all classes, but especially among the underprivileged and the young—attests to the speed of change and the need of adaptation to meet it.

As to the long-run requirements for a prosperous, just, and

free Atlantic Community, we can do no better than quote the United States Declaration of Independence, signed almost two centuries ago. It captured the best inspirations of that time in Europe and brought them to the new world which was then emerging in effect as a "United Europe."

We hold these truths to be self-evident, that all men are created equal, that they are endowed by their Creator with certain inalienable Rights, that among these are Life, Liberty, and the Pursuit of Happiness. That to secure these rights, governments are instituted among Men, deriving their just powers from the consent of the governed.

These truths are as self-evident today as they were when written. Certainly to assure life, liberty, and the pursuit of happiness or, in more modern words, security, freedom, and opportunity for all, are still the basic responsibilities of government today. Yet how can any government fulfill these responsibilities in this crowded, interdependent, nuclear, jet-propelled, technological, automated, computerized, accelerating, and incredibly complex world of today and tomorrow?

With the geometrically growing impingement of all these factors on our lives, it is small wonder that institutions are lagging behind, while we grope for new and better means of dealing with change, of encouraging its beneficial effects, and of countering injurious ones.

It was no coincidence that the nation-state evolved soon after gunpowder came into wide use in the West. It served us reasonably well during the gunpowder age. What will serve as well, or better, in the nuclear age?

The burgeoning of problems everywhere makes it inevitable that all governments are increasingly preoccupied with their own domestic crises and problems, with a corresponding desire for disengagement from other countries' problems. Yet are these problems primarily national, or more properly human? Similarities in human beings, economic and cultural interdependence, and almost instantaneous worldwide communications make them far wider than national. Similar factors and the same restlessness, operating mostly under the surface in Communist nations, may in more distant time open up the possibility of new perspectives for gradual liberalization and increasing East-West collaboration.

There is widespread disillusionment with traditional militarism, nationalism, politics, and politicians. There is questioning of the adequacy of governmental procedures for dealing with domestic and foreign problems in the United States, United Kingdom, France, Germany and Italy, Eastern Europe, and elsewhere. We have all watched on TV student uprisings from Rio and Mexico City to Berkeley, Cambridge, and New York; from London, Paris, Berlin, and Rome to Belgrade, Prague, Warsaw, Tokyo, New Delhi, and Peking. These can hardly be dismissed as pure coincidence. Underlying it all appears a search for individual identity— a longing for dignity, security, and opportunity. Those who have little want the opportunity to enjoy more material things and dignity. The affluent want these also and both want something more—idealism, purpose, fulfillment—they do not exactly know what. And everywhere is a pervasive nostalgia for simplicity.

Business and People on the Move

Meanwhile, amid disappointment and frustration and the restlessness of youth, certain developments of portentous implications for the future have been occurring under our noses.

International business, without waiting for political development, has spilled over national boundaries to bring new inventions, new technology, new management ideas, and new prosperity to millions of people—especially in the Atlantic area. To finance this surge of enterprise, the money managers of Europe and North America and Japan and elsewhere have been learning to work together, and in the process they have designed new instruments to help the monetary machinery to serve the people better.

While this has been going on, the people of the West have developed new concepts and means of travel. They have swarmed by the millions into other countries, bringing home new perspectives and wider horizons. Travel for study holds the promise of ultimately building up a new international elite with new ideas for our civilization. Travel, science, and education in combination have awakened most of us to the need and the possibility for improvement in man's whole environment of land, air, water, communications, and standards of habitation. And with this awakening has come a new stirring of conscience over the condition of the less-developed countries and their insistent demand to share in the good life.

Revolution of Technology

Technological change in our interdependent world has become cumulative, to the extent that it has become prudent to expect the unexpected.

It is said that of all the people who have ever lived, two per cent are alive today, but that of all the scientists who have ever lived, ninety per cent are now alive. Not only are we in the early years of a scientific age, but new knowledge is disseminated more widely and more rapidly than ever before.

Research has become subject to organized mass production and computers have revolutionized the storage and retrieval of information for the solving of complex problems. Further acceleration seems a safe prediction; and yet we have still to learn how to deal effectively with the human and social problems being created by technology, or how to harness technology to deal with these new problems and those left over from an earlier age.

These new activities and new ideas have spawned a revolt against the slowness of change in every aspect of society. This in itself is a wind of change with both good and dangerous implications, such as its dramatic impact on youth. These vast changes require new political frameworks and the setting aside of many old concepts and machinery. New institutions must grow out of the new economic and social realities.

Thus the 70's will inevitably bring an increasingly crowded planet, increasingly interdependent, its problems increasingly complex. The two basic trends—the quest for the larger political and economic units necessary to deal with today's problems, and that for greater human fulfillment and equality of opportunity—will surely continue. Divergent national *interests* will decline in importance compared to wider common interests, but diverse local and national *values* will be increasingly prized.

How can we devise and build the better institutions we need and create the better society which is in our grasp? How can the American people and their Government, with their unparalleled affluence and power, best contribute, beset as they are with grave problems at home and abroad?

NEW APPROACHES

Because of this welter of changes, this book seeks to approach its analyses of the European-American question in a new way. Instead of the classic division of the subject into military, economic, and political, it begins by a discussion of the human problems involved: the revolt by youth, the impatience with conventional solutions, restiveness of the "third world," the effect of science on human problems. In these areas the pot has boiled up in the past few years and promises to boil more as the decade advances.

We cannot hope to estimate the future simply by an extrapolation or projection of the trends of even the recent past. We must try to throw into the equation some of the new and unexpected developments.

So this book starts with an attempt to appraise the reactions of the new generation. They are the people who will shape events in the years to come. It recognizes a new perspective in Europe with the stepping down of General de Gaulle and a revival of hope for European unity, which would narrow the gap between Europe and America. Still further, account must be taken of new interest in the struggle with man's environment accented by President Nixon's proposals to NATO.

All these considerations lead to an attempt to appraise the new framework for European-North American relations within which the more traditional activities may be examined.

We hope that the reader may find that this approach will prove a stimulus to thought and add a useful perspective to these vital problems.

—LIVINGSTON T. MERCHANT

PART I

The Atlantic Society

Since Europeans first set foot on Caribbean shores, the social principles and customs of the Mother Continent have shaped American thinking and practices profoundly. As the settlers began to develop an identity and perspective of their own, the Atlantic became a two-way street for intellectual and not-so-intellectual exchange. Thanks to television and other instant media, fashions in ideas and life-styles now jump the Atlantic with the speed of light, and people follow with only slightly less speed.

In a few short years, the Atlantic has become to the culture of the modern world what the Mediterranean was to the Ancients. The 1970's will see the general flowering of cultural interdependence among the peoples around the Atlantic basin. It is not too soon to speak of an Atlantic society.

Although this Atlantic society or community is often thought of only-or mostly-in economic and political terms, it is much more than that. It is a changing, pulsing, breathing life organism.

But now, just when the countries of the community have achieved new and astounding growth and prosperity, their society is shaken by a widespread revolt among the younger generation.

At the same time the community has awakened to the fact that its whole environment is being gradually poisoned by pollution of air and water and the by-products of industry.

So any look ahead must first take account of these cultural changes.

CHAPTER 1

Youth and Atlantic Society

A nation is no more than a constantly changing stream of persons who, having experienced and decided, give way to strangers to both the experience and the decision. Constancy is the result of continued relearning and faith.

DEAN ACHESON[1]

By a strange paradox today's ferment of youth appears to be a by-product of success in achieving some of the most sought after objectives of Western man: mass education, relative leisure, mobility—both physical and social—and increased affluence. Along with these new freedoms have come new modes of communication—especially television, with its display of violence—and an awakened concern over social injustices.

In the United States, confrontation with a detested military obligation has brought unrest to a head. The combination of influences has become explosive, not in the United States alone but nearly world-wide. The causes are broad, deep, and varied.

Aside from its invitation to chaos, the feeling of revolt by many young people interposes a roadblock in the way of the transmission to their generation of the accumulated wisdom of experience.

[1] *Present at the Creation.* New York: W. W. Norton & Co., 1969. p. 489.

On the positive side the uprising represents a new and welcome interest of youth in political and international problems which, if tempered by knowledge and experience, can carry fresh hope for the future.

Patterns of Discontent[2]

While a majority of the youth in Western countries seems moderate, orderly and content to make their way within the existing system, a considerable number do not fit this pattern. Youthwatchers keep an eye on three groups:

(a) passivists, comprising drop-outs from the real world, who represent in some measure the inroads of drug addiction.

(b) activists who want revolution for its own sake. It is they whom society mostly fears, a minority of young radicals who are in step with a hardy tradition of anarchism and violence and who are fascinated by the process of rebellion.

(c) a third and much larger group, the activists with serious causes, and respect for democratic processes. They have much of the sympathy of old-style liberals and others who advocate fundamental social and economic changes. But these sincere young reformers sometimes succumb to the siren call of the militant radicals for instant action and are lured by their myths and slogans. They are unfortunately often confused with the revolutionaries, and are often blamed for their excesses. They in turn succeed at times in arousing to action the moderate and normally quiet majority.

It is important to be clear about what is at stake. Even though few of us a bare half-decade ago could have believed it possible, the fundamental political beliefs of Western industrial society are being challenged on a wide front. No one could honestly say that the political institutions of any Atlantic country are yet "at bay," but if present trends continue towards social alienation of substantial groups, coupled with

[2]This analysis is based on an unpublished report prepared by Mr. Huntley for the North Atlantic Assembly, Brussels.

mounting violence and a progressive radicalization of politics at both ends of the spectrum, then the Atlantic civic culture could be set back for decades. At the very least, these movements are diverting vast thought and energy from other important affairs of life.

The dissidence of many youth, and concurrent demands of the underprivileged, have given rise to what has been termed the "new politics." Even though so far the movement is strong among only a minority, it threatens, at least potentially, the West's ideals, its political institutions, its embryonic international community.

The real danger in these trends was summarized recently by a German observer of the political scene:

Conditions are ripe for all kinds of false prophets. Some believe police clubs are the way to create order. Others proclaim the unconditional and absolute freedom of mankind . . . What about the threats of violence that lie behind all present events? We can no longer pretend to be naïve. A utopia of totally liberated people who are responsible solely to themselves, released from all social ties but also social commitments, leads not to freedom but to a state of uncaged animality, and always creates an option for a minority to exercise terror and impose on a reluctant majority its idea of universal happiness. [3]

The Roots of Discontent

There has always been a generation gap, but today in a number of countries it seems to be widening seriously. For what they are worth, there follow here some of the thoughts of serious people as to the special causes.

The width of the generation gap is partly due to a failure to transmit to the new generation an understanding of the extraordinary developments of the war and post-war decades. Today's adults know that, for all its faults, Western society has come a long way indeed in thirty or forty years;

[3] Giselher Wirsing, "After de Gaulle," *Christ Und Welt,* May 24, 1968 (reprinted in *Atlas,* July, 1968, p. 25).

but youth generally seems to believe that the "system" and the "establishment," which define the bounds for everyone, have changed little.

The psychological impact of widespread affluence has been profound on both the affluent and the needy. The latter's rising expectations cannot be satisfied fast enough; the former are rebelling against materialistic gods, embodied in the "consumer society." James Reston recently wrote, "Part of the tumult of the age is precisely that men no longer regard slavery and poverty as inevitable but intolerable."[4]

The affluence of the modern West has opened up options for youth that no earlier generation ever had. Today's young people have freedom to travel, to delay careers, to stop studying if they wish. And yet, while young people have a great range of choices for their future, the military draft is interposed as a rude awakening.

Although they are the beneficiaries of affluence, many youths rebel at its manifestation. They are not content with the treatment by society of those who do not share in the affluence. There is disgust with the hypocrisies of society and with the obvious gulf between the ideals of adults and their performance. (Let it also be said that in their profound discontent with what industrial society has done to the world, young people are not alone; many older people are discouraged by the lack of responsiveness and flexibility of both leaders and institutions.)

The Penalty of Permissiveness

Some would ascribe the youthful revolt to the latter-day permissiveness of schools and parents, spurred on by such teachings as those of Dewey and Spock. Permissiveness gone overboard probably contributes to the frustration of American youth when they come up against entrenched authority in universities and business.[5] But the liberating

---

[4] *The New York Times*, August 16, 1968.
[5] *Fortune* (January, 1969, p. 173) quotes evidence, from a poll of American youth attitudes, that student activists "tend to come from 'democratic' homes in which children are encouraged to speak up."

ideas of Dewey and Spock still figure relatively little in the child-rearing practices of most of the European continent, where nevertheless revolt has also taken place.

Although it is likely that theories of education and their practical applications must play some role in the youth rebellion, the actual casual relationship is less than clear. The great differences between American and European theory and practice in this important field suggest that the matter is more complicated than the popular press would suggest.

Nor can the youth rebellion be laid solely at the door of television. The mass media, and particularly TV, have certainly played a part by giving the various uprisings and lesser incidents more public attention than they deserve, by broadcasting evocative—sometimes incendiary—pictures of violence and destruction. But long before television or radio or the other apparatus of instant public affairs existed, the Western revolutions of 1848 swept all of Europe like wildfire, growing similarily out of a widespread revulsion against the "powers" and the "systems" of that day.

The roots of discontent are clearly deeper than even the tentacles of the mass media can reach.

Left-Wing Influence

It is tempting to try to lay the blame for both youth and racial disorders on sinister left-wing forces, Communist or otherwise. While the Soviets and the Red Chinese, or the Fidelistas, are not above giving judicious support or training to rebellious student groups or older agitators, no convincing evidence has so far been uncovered to trace the widespread unrest to a Communist plot. There are some hard left-wing intellectual strains visible in the youth rebellion (some so far left as to be anathema to the Kremlin) and some recognizable influences, including Marx and Mao, from the past and present; but nearly all of these influences can be likened to intellectual matches thrown into a mass of explosively dry tinder.

If world Communism has had an influence on the youth rebellion, it is more likely to be found in Kremlin (and Western) policies of coexistence and "détente," which, following the Cuban crisis in 1962, gave rise to the widespread belief that the West is no longer beleaguered by international Communism, and hence is freer to indulge its own forces of selfishness and disorder.

Today's youth in large part simply do not accept the conclusions of their elders about where we have been and where we are going. They did not live through the Depression, or watch Hitler come near to world domination, or feel the chilling shadow of Stalinist Communism, waiting to pick up the pieces when western Europe would collapse from its economic decimation and rickety social patchwork.

The Search for Self-Determination

When Adolf Hitler, and later Stalin, confronted the West, the societies of the Atlantic nations set aside their internal difficulties to present a solid front in the face of grave external danger. Every country, to a greater or lesser extent, postponed urgently needed domestic renovations, and now the chickens are coming home to roost. These accumulated social problems and injustices are today compounded by the impact of science on society. Because we have given our youth better education than we had, and because a much greater number today have both the time and the inclination for education, they have acquired an insatiable thirst for self-determination. There is a sense everywhere, not only among youth, that change is essential, that things cannot stay as they are. Flora Lewis, in commenting on the French Revolution of 1968, said:

It was not so much specific burdens or personalities—not even the person of de Gaulle—that people wanted to change. They wanted, rather, a sense of being able to cause change when and how it came to be needed, and in the accepted, traditional way.[6]

[6] "The Demise of the French Left," *Saturday Review*, August 10, 1968, p. 20.

More than ever before—and this is entirely in keeping with the spirit of the Atlantic Idea—people want to think and act *for themselves,* rather than to be leaves in the wind, given to whatever fate a vast, amorphous, mindless society has in store for them. Everyone wants an *individual identity* —and nearly everyone today believes that he *can* have one. Neither the awakened youth nor the dispossessed of our time are willing to settle for drabness, or anonymity, or domination by others, or wars over which one has no control.

One of the prophets of radical youth is an obscure Ger- man-born sociologist, Herbert Marcuse.[7]

His writings may be misled and misleading, negative, un- clear, destructive, and even incendiary, but there is in them a kernel of important truth: the Western way of life *does* tend to gloss over its shortcomings, to condition the common man to ignore or accept them.

Thus one can sympathize to a large extent with the roots of today's discontent, for some of the concern is a healthy sign and many of the activists' goals are worthy. But it is the growing number of totalitarians among the discontented, and equally among those who fear them and who fear change, which constitutes a grave danger to the West. The center, on which civic health has always depended, is today being squeezed—dangerously—by the wings.

Transatlantic Phenomenon

Students in Berlin, putting the torch to publisher Axel Springer's delivery trucks, shouted, "Burn, baby, burn!" From the Free Speech Movement at Berkeley, from "Red Rudi," to "Danny the Red," from Herbert Marcuse to Chica- go's Lincoln Park and the faculties of Nanterre, the slender fuses run. The thrill of being part of a conspiracy, of making common cause with the oppressed, of printing clandestine literature, and of "striking a blow for freedom," has spread

[7] Perhaps the most complete statement of Marcuse's philosophy is contained in his *One Dimensional Man* (London: Routledge and Kegan Paul) 1964.

contagiously from one part of the Western world to another, sometimes overnight. The interconnection seems to be largely one of ideas and a relatively few leaders, not systematically organized or financed.

The "new politics," whether stemming from the youth rebellion, the indignation of the American Negro, or the unrest of the working population in many European countries, is now a general transatlantic phenomenon. This "new politics" is vitally important to every Atlantic country because it could conceivably bring about profound, unwelcome changes in the social and political systems.

It is important also because the youthful energy and attention which is going into these causes, some (but clearly not all) of them unrealistic or positively unworthy, are needed to revitalize the Atlantic system's own international transformation and to attack even deeper domestic problems (most of them widespread in the Atlantic community) in a common cause with those who now hold the levers of power.

The new politics is also important to the Atlantic countries because they will be forced to turn inward to deal with domestic discontent if they cannot soon contain it, and this could mean postponement or even conceivably the end of meaningful efforts to bring an integrated political and economic Atlantic system to fruition in our time.

A Lesson of History

After World War I there was a general revulsion, a rejection of the war's results, a misreading of its causes, and an attempt to rewrite history, *especially by those who hadn't been through it.* This misguided "idealism" reached the height of irresponsibility at Oxford and Cambridge in the 1930's, leaving Britain morally unprepared for the holocaust to come.

Most of those who now, with violence, demand radical changes in "the system" are totally uncoupled from the history of the past three decades. The belief in and the development of an Atlantic community of peoples rest on a sound historical conception of what the West has lived through in the past fifty years. If one were to liquidate these historical judgments, then we should be left with no base for coherent international—or national—policies on the present continuum. But most of those deeply involved in the "new politics" are either ignorant of recent history or don't think it matters.

Student Opinions on International Questions

What do students believe about international affairs? By and large, today's young people are internationalists and humanitarians. Their parents concentrated on East-West relations, but youth worry about the North-South axis and the ecology of our planet. They know they will have to deal with overpopulation, underdevelopment, and rampant technology long after we are gone.

Many of the young appear to believe the Cold War is over and that freedom from nuclear conflict may be taken largely for granted. A recent study in several countries[8] showed a majority of youth willing to dissolve NATO in return for dissolution of the Warsaw Pact. To the extent that NATO is supported, most young people seem to think its business is to play a peaceful role, promote more détente, and work itself out of business.

As the goal for European youth, western European unification no longer suffices. It is considered largely a technical, even old-fashioned, idea. In any case, change-minded European youth are asking whether a federal Europe would not simply result in the same poor-quality society on a much larger scale. There is less inclination than formerly to see a united Europe (and even less an Atlantic community) as a logical next step toward world community. One could—and should—pass at once to "one world" without war; this is a recurring theme among youth.

European students identify with the United States less

8 By Vincent Joyce for the Atlantic Treaty Association, Paris, unpublished, 1967.

than formerly. In a 1969 opinion study,[9] more than two-thirds of the students at the College of Europe said that "the United States constitutes a society distinct from that of Europe and does not foreshadow the image of a future Europe." Asked the same question about the USSR, a lesser number (but still a majority) felt estranged.

At an Atlantic Institute conference in 1968 a young Englishman observed that "Vietnam had an essential impact on student revolt in the West; young people say they do not want this kind of America to speak for all of the West." On every side, there is evidence that large numbers of American as well as European youth want greater independence of Europe from the United States

As yet, there appear to be no organized "anti-NATO" or "anti-Europe" movements among the young, but in 1970 protests against NATO began to surface in Western Europe.

WHAT CAN BE DONE?

The cardinal questions are these:

—Can those who now hold the reins of leadership successfully transmit an intellectually sound, undistorted conception of history to those who will lead in the future?

—Can the remaining blots on the West's escutcheon—the lingering pockets of social injustice of which youth is so conscious—be attacked with more convincing programs?

—Can we successfully modify our educational institutions from elementary school on, so that they are more flexible and more responsive, more democratic and more in tune with the times, so that youth have a livelier sense of participation and relevance?

—Can adult leadership capture the imagination and enthusiasm of young activists who are genuinely interested in reform? Furthermore, can they successfully add to this cross-generation coalition significant numbers from among those youth—no doubt a majority—whose political attitudes

[9] Leo Moulin, "*The Young and Europe,*" College of Europe, 1969.

are moderate or quiescent, but who represent potentially a constructive force?

International Objectives

In the area of international policy the European idea caught fire among youth fifteen and twenty years ago, but their enthusiasm began to wane when De Gaulle first vetoed British entry into the Common Market. Today those clouds are lifting and once more there is a possibility of making European unity an attractive cause. This is not easy because the "making of Europe" has become a highly technocratic process, largely out of public sight.

American students were never really set afire with the Atlantic idea. In 1939 and 1940, a few were aroused by Clarence Streit to champion "Union Now," and a handful have never lost their faith and ardor. But generally speaking, NATO and OECD and American support for the unity of Europe are things that the entire American population, youth included, have until recently generally accepted matter-of-factly as being both desirable and necessary, but were not ideas they had absorbed into their emotional concept of things worth fighting for.

That poses exactly the problem. For youth are idealistic, and search for causes to which they can give their great energy, intelligence, and enthusiasm. It should be possible to light a torch for a feeling of common destiny between America and Europe and an appreciation of the importance of the Atlantic system's institution-building over the past two decades as both a practical model and a powerful force for a world without war.[10]

Another international problem for which youth have shown their concern, commitment, and good will is the plight of the less developed countries. The Peace Corps and similar organizations in several European countries have

[10] *Fortune* January, 1969, (p. 92) observed: "Often accused by their offspring of not practicing what they preach, the parents of today's young adults failed to preach what they practiced."

provided convincing evidence of the strength of this appeal, both overseas and domestically. The idea of youthful service caught on, although it has lost the first flush of enthusiasm.

A related subject of wide international implications in which youth everywhere has shown interest is the mounting danger to man's environment.

Could not a substantial further effort be organized among the youth of Atlantic countries to work on social develop- ment or ecological projects inside and outside the Atlantic system, building on the experience already accumulated?

In a larger sense, this sort of volunteer service program would seek to develop one set of answers to a problem that will loom large in the 1970's and beyond: what happens after the new post-industrial economy has automated to the nth degree, the hours of work have fallen dramatically, and the per capita GNP has risen remarkably? How does West- ern man then occupy himself? Is the removal of work-pres- sure to be replaced by aimlessness, alienation, mass lethargy, bread-and-circuses, protest and violence? Or could orga- nized help to less-developed nations and to those hand- icapped in the West help to answer those who ask for a purpose in life?

Since the youth revolt began to assume alarming propor- tions in 1968, older people in the Atlantic countries have begun to think and—in some cases—act seriously about it. The Council of Europe's parliamentary assembly held a fas- cinating debate in September, 1968, on the subject, as did the North Atlantic Assembly a year later. Most countries have initiated parliamentary and other investigations, and in some cases legislation and programs to deal with legitimate complaints.

Youth themselves, in the United States, began their own "movement for decency" in 1969. Some young Frenchmen not long ago started a "JFK Club" to seek ideals, construc- tive leadership, and brotherhood; they were deluged with requests from all over Europe for aid in starting similar groups. In the United States, Britain, France, Italy, and many

other countries vigorous attempts by students and others are
under way to bring needed reforms to the universities.

In the Spring of 1969, while the radical minority was
occupying university administration buildings or disrupting
classes in far-flung places, the students of the Federal Institute of Technology, at Zurich, organized a public petition,
secured the holding of a national referendum, and cam-
paigned successfully to defeat a new federal law regulating
engineering schools, which they believed to be against the
students' interests. They demonstrated how political ends
can be achieved by using the established processes.

In 1970 in the United States, many students have been
active in congressional campaigns across the country, working "within the system."

Equal Burdens in Public Service

To have raised the question of peaceful service by Western youth is automatically to raise a second, directly related
question: military service in defense of the Atlantic system.
At this stage in history, the armed might of the Atlantic
system is essential to our survival.

The Vietnam War, whatever its defects or virtues, has
badly hurt the Atlantic system in a number of ways. Not least
has been the effect it has had on the readiness of American
youth to serve in the country's defense forces. Many young
men, while quite ready to fight for the "basic survival" of the
United States find it difficult, faced with the Vietnam War,
to let their government decide when and where that survival is at stake and their military services needed.

The U. S. selective service system, in facing these unusual
responsibilities, has operated in ways regarded by many as
unfair. One answer by a responsible commission is the shift
to a volunteer army.[11] Another alternative would be to develop universal service—including perhaps an optional
"Peace Corps" type of civil substitute—for all youth, plus a

[11] Report to the President of Advisory Commission on a Volunteer Armed Force,
Thomas Gates, Chairman, Feb. 21, 1970.

highly professional standing army adequate to manage limited regional conflicts. France has set a partial example of this sort with optional civilian service abroad in place of military service.

As the NATO countries have no common policy with respect to national service, this is a valid question for joint Atlantic study. If rightly conceived, for the right purposes, and explained in the right ways, universal service could educate and even inspire young people.

New Directions of Education

These specific proposals of course must be conceived as part of a broad program of education of youth for a changed and changing world. Neither in the United States nor the other Atlantic countries have the educational systems kept pace with new international relationships and responsibilities.

In some directions great progress has been made. One of the most beneficial influences has been vastly increased contacts among peoples, including students, due to travel. For the United States new vistas were opened in World War II by service abroad of eleven million American men and women, from every city and town. Since then there has been a steadily increasing flow of people back and forth across the oceans—governmental, congressional, business, tourist, academic, and student. Each year some 130,000 foreign students come to United States schools, colleges, and universities and some 30,000 Americans go abroad to study.

In this process the young acquire new concepts, but too often they get them incidentally and by osmosis more than through teaching directly geared to the contemporary world scene. There is room, and need, for a major updating and synthesizing of history, economics and political science, and their relation to contemporary problems of the technological age. This involves major changes in course content, and preparation and reorientation of the teacher.

The traditional style and methods of education, and of diplomacy for that matter, are inadequate with respect particularly to relations between the partners of the Atlantic system, who have entered a new age of multilateral community.

TO SUM UP

The Atlantic society is suffering from a strange paradox of affluence. At a time of great prosperity, a wave of discontent, led by youth, has swept the nations on both sides of the Atlantic.

Among the roots of the trouble is a wide generation gap, accentuated by difference in experience. Youth did not go through and does not appreciate the struggles, apprehensions and achievements of the war and post-war period. And somehow today's elders have failed to communicate adequately their experiences and conclusions.

Today's youth are freer to think and to choose and to act than any of their predecessors. They see more clearly, perhaps, defects, injustices, evils which their elders too often take for granted.

Some of the youth, a minority, are the reincarnation of anarchism; they want to disrupt and destroy.

Some, again a minority, are dropouts and passivists, in many cases victims of drugs.

The majority are serious, idealistic, humanitarian, but restless and concerned.

The widespread unrest of youth is enormously important for the future of Western civilization. It could disrupt and seriously hamper the flow of sound education. It could arouse the repressive instincts of more conservative people and feed a new isolationism.

On the other hand it could, if given the right guidance and direction, produce a renaissance in human, political, and economic relationships across frontiers.

The road to meet this dilemma would seem to lie, first, in unending effort to establish better communication between the young and the older generation.

The most direct responsibility, after the home, falls on the schools and colleges, which are finding they must give students much more participation and responsibility and must seek more realism in curricula, and more freedom in student life, while at the same time discovering the line at which firm discipline begins, and learning how to apply it.

National policies are a major factor in this equation. The Vietnam tragedy overhangs student life in the United States and, to a surprising extent, abroad. Also there is a general student desire to move faster in integration of minorities. For these, solutions must become more convincing.

But above all, young people must be drawn into causes which will arouse their enthusiasms. It should be possible to capture the interest and imagination of the students in international problems and projects, which in their turn are in fact closely related to the concerns and opportunities of daily life.

CHAPTER 2

Shaping Our Environment: An Atlantic Problem

Nowhere do we have any body of thinkers whose duty it is to take all those things—the air, the water, the land, population, the environment—and put them together. We must do this because, for the first time, the planet is one. For the first time man has looked on the earth from the outside and he has seen how small and fragile it is.[1]

MARGARET MEAD

In our first chapter, we examined the new political discontents and disruptive cultural currents, centering particularly around youth, which are sweeping the societies around the North Atlantic basin (although by no means confined to them). This chapter is devoted to another way of looking at Atlantic society: its environment.

The impact of technology and affluence on the environment and the social structures of our countries is profound. People everywhere are increasingly worried about the quality of their physical surroundings. It is entirely possible that our world—and the Atlantic system in its vanguard—could some day become worthless as a place of habitation for humans.

[1] *The New York Times*, May 3, 1970, p. 30.

31

THE WORLD ENVIRONMENTAL CRISIS

The crisis is world wide and has three main components: headlong, universal urbanization; the population explosion; and the damaging encroachment of man's technologies on his physical and socio-cultural surroundings.

Technology now threatens the ecological balance of the globe. The rising curve of scientific and technological change makes the impossible possible and previously non-dangerous situations explosive. Humanity has never before, all at once, had to deal with such forces of social, cultural, economic, and political change as at present.

If current population trends continue to the beginning of the next century, the present 3½ billion human beings on the planet will have about doubled. Population could double again by 2040.[2]

As technological innovation takes over in agriculture, the farm population of the Atlantic countries has moved inexorably into the urban areas, where the jobs and the attractions of city life are to be found. Many of the current pressures on American cities, for example, can be traced to the headlong pace of this internal migration over the last two decades.

Although a few scientists and other watchful persons have warned of an impending environmental crisis, publics and governments did not become truly alarmed until 1969. In the summer of that year, pollution killed 40 million fish in the Rhine. Massive oil leakage fouled the ocean beaches off California, in Britain, and in France. DDT, a cheap, effective pesticide which had done much to raise world food production, was shown to have harmed the life cycles of a wide range of the world's living creatures, including man. Levels of air pollution in industrial areas and large cities were pronounced unsafe. Even noise was coming to be regarded as a form of pollution.

Because of tremendous population growth, the rapid movement into urban areas, and the deleterious effects of

[2] *Brittanica Book of the Year*, 1968, p. 25.

technological "progress" on the conditions of life, planners in many countries cannot "freeze" the situation long enough to make a rational plan.

Environmental planning and control, to be effective in many cases, must transcend national borders. Ocean pollution, for example, is a global problem. Neither air pollution control measures nor land-use planning in northwest Europe, for example, can any longer be done by nations acting singly. In this case, regional planning by a group of countries is called for. Constantinos A. Doxiadis, a pioneer in ekistics (the science of human settlements) forecasts a "city of the whole inhabited earth" in a few short generations.[3] The process of urbanization cannot be stopped, but somehow, and soon, if life in cities is not to become completely inhuman, adequate planning must take hold. In many respects, it must be international in scope. At the very least, urban planners and administrators stand to learn a good deal if regular interchanges of experience can be devised.

INTERNATIONAL EFFORTS TO MANAGE THE ENVIRONMENT

With public concern mounting swiftly, various international organizations entered the lists in 1969 against the forces of environmental deterioration.

In a remarkable report to the Economic and Social Council of the U. N., in May 1969, Secretary General U Thant portrayed the extraordinary dangers to man's environment. Numerous scientific and technical studies are in process under U. N. auspices. UNESCO made environment its major topic for 1969, and the U. N. General Assembly authorized a global conference on the subject at Stockholm for 1972.

The European Communities in March 1969 proposed a series of environment activities for joint pursuit by the Six, some in cooperation with other European countries and the

[3] *Op. Cit.*, p. 34.

United States. The Council of Europe, which has mounted several studies on pollution and protection of cultural treasures endangered by environmental pressures, held a conference on nature conservation in February 1970 which drew world attention. The Nordic Council, composed of the Scandinavian countries and Finland, also put environmental studies on its agenda.

The OECD, too, has entered the environment field in a number of practical ways. In one month (September 1969), for example, OECD held meetings of research groups on "the unintended occurrence of pesticides," "water management," "lighting, visibility, and accidents," and "area traffic control systems."

In February 1970, OECD announced its intention to work out international tolerance limits for pollutants. Countries exceeding limits would pay indemnities. At the same time, OECD's Secretary General, Emile Van Lennep, declared that the Organization intended to "introduce a qualitative factor into its studies on economic growth. In other words, growth in social as well as economic terms will be studied" by OECD's staff.[4]

NATO AND THE ENVIRONMENT

To some extent, it appears that OECD's new plans may have been a response to earlier initiatives in still another "Atlantic" body, the North Atlantic Treaty Organization. Set up originally as a multinational military deterrent and a political instrument for eventual resolution of the Cold War, NATO entered the environment game in the summer of 1969. How did it happen and why?

President Nixon, on April 10, 1969, recommended to the foreign ministers of the NATO nations the creation of a special NATO committee on the "challenges of modern society . . . to explore ways in which the experience and resources of the Western nations could most effectively be

[4] *The New York Times,* February 18, 1970.

marshalled toward improving the quality of life of our peoples."

This seemed to be recognition that the common concerns of the West are not limited to military or economic or political matters but, as the President put it, to other deeply relevant problems, "the legitimate unrest of our young people, the frustration of the gap between generations, the need for a new sense of idealism and purpose in coping with an automated world."

Apparently this proposal for an unusual activity in NATO was a novel thought to most of the foreign ministers and their governments. NATO's Secretary General, Manlio Brosio, traveled from capital to capital in the summer which followed to sound out views on what, if anything, ought to be done to pursue the President's suggestion. There were differences of opinion. Some governments reportedly were opposed to any environmental role for NATO; others were favorable but unsure as to how the Organization could carve out a meaningful, coherent series of activities without duplicating the work of others. Some officials believed that NATO should restrict itself to technological issues, citing NATO's prior experience, over two decades, in promoting scientific research and a massive transfer of technology among nations. Finally, there was considerable reticence on financial grounds; would not this sort of open-ended activity cost large sums of money?

Except in one or two cases, the response to the President's plea for a third dimension to NATO's work was more acquiescent than enthusiastic. Discussions, however, began in Brussels around NATO's green tables.

Only in November 1969, when the North Atlantic Council decided to form a Committee on the Challenges of Modern Society (CCMS), did the member governments begin to realize that they had seized a vital, exciting set of issues. NATO was riding a wave of aroused public opinion which covered at least the advanced world.

A press communique stated the Committee's charge:

How to improve, in every practical way, the exchange of views and experience among the Allied Countries in the task of creating a better environment for their society. It will consider specific problems of the human environment with the deliberate objective of stimulating action by member governments.

By mid-December, when the Committee held its first meeting, both the NATO Secretariat and the national delegations, for the most part, were inclined to take the "third dimension" seriously.

President Nixon, to indicate the importance which he attached to the new effort, appointed as U.S. Representative to the committee, Daniel P. Moynihan, a top-ranking White House official dealing with social affairs. Several other NATO governments responded in kind.

Two concepts are pivotal to the work of the new Committee, as the Secretary General explained on December 10, 1969:

1. The first is the *pilot country* idea. One country, possibly in association with other members, would be actually responsible for a study which CCMS decided to undertake.

2. The second idea is that efforts will not be directed towards research, but towards questions of *government policy formulation* and *legislation*. The NATO nations will be invited by the pilot countries to consider ways and means of action (on the basis of available scientific, technical, and economic studies) susceptible to bring about improvements to the physical and social environment.

At its first meeting CCMS decided that social as well as technological problems of the environment would be covered by the NATO studies. CCMS was also discussed as a means of sparking concrete cooperation between NATO members and countries of eastern Europe, though the OECD or the UN Economic Commission for Europe might be more acceptable agencies for this purpose. It was also agreed that CCMS activities, unlike most other deliberations of NATO, would be unclassified and open to full publicity and public scrutiny. Finally, a policy was adopted to make CCMS environmental studies, once adopted by the North Atlantic Council, available to all public authorities, and not only in NATO member countries.

Initial pilot studies included road safety (U. S.); disaster relief (U. S., Italy co-pilots); air pollution (U. S., Germany and Turkey co-pilots); open waters pollution (Belgium, Portugal co-pilots); inland water pollution (Canada, U.S. and France co-pilots); regional planning and ecology (France). While these were largely technological in nature, two other studies had particular social and political import: The United Kingdom agreed to pilot a study on "the problems of individual and group motivations in a modern industrial society—with the emphasis on individual fulfillment." The Federal Republic of Germany began consideration of "the problem of the transmission of scientific knowledge to the decision-making sectors of government.[5] In explaining his government's commitment to this study and to the general work of CCMS, Professor Ralf Dahrendorf of Germany told fellow committee members:

The very fact that this Committee has been created shows that for us, security depends as much on the vitality of our societies as it does on the strength of our armies.

For all these apparently positive developments, some critics nevertheless fear that this new activity may somehow dilute NATO's main purpose, which is seen as defense. Still others believe that other organizations, such as UNESCO or OECD or the Council of Europe, would be more appropriate in this new role.

Yet officials and NATO-watchers in Brussels point out that Article 2 of the North Atlantic Treaty, which broadly

[5] *NATO Latest No. 10*, NATO Information Service, December 10, 1969, pp. 1–2.

pledged the parties to "promote conditions of stability and well-being" among their peoples, clearly provided for activity of this kind. They say, too, that NATO through the years has actually become a highly versatile political instrument. If such procedures as the "NATO Annual Review" of national defense plans were applied to environmental fields, for example, surprising benefits might result.

Still others argue that for two decades NATO has carried on, at ever-increasing levels of complexity, a massive system of technology transfer, not only in military matters but in broader scientific efforts. To the extent that technology is *the* environmental issue, NATO would seem uniquely qualified.

Finally, say defenders of the third dimension idea, NATO's members take the Alliance seriously. NATO's findings in environmental questions will probably get high-level attention. There appears to be some evidence to support this view: NATO governments apparently realized, in the process of organizing their own participation in CCMS, that they may not have been paying sufficient attention to the broad range of ecological problems as a single complex worthy of consideration at the highest levels of public concern. Six governments, including the German and the French, were moved, after CCMS's creation, to organize their own cabinet working groups to look at the way they are responding across the board to the environmental challenges of modern society.

SHAPING THE ENVIRONMENT AS A LONG-RANGE INTERNATIONAL TASK

This kind of activity could conceivably turn out to be a major new feature of the Atlantic society in the 1970's. With some successes, CCMS could turn NATO into a demonstrably constructive, even popular, force. Conversely, CCMS could result in NATO falling on its collective face, for it is usually several times more difficult to organize effectively on an international scale than within one government, in peaceful as well as military fields.

Central to the hopes for such cooperative programs is the proposition that no single nation has many of the answers to the accelerating problems of modern society, but that each might know more than some, or occasionally all, of the others in a given sphere of public activity. The Swedish invention of the Ombudsman, now adopted in one form or another in at least a dozen other countries, is a case in point.

Practical Steps

The more technological problems, such as pollution, nutrition, the deterioration of transport, and the decay of housing, lend themselves in most instances to the application of modern scientific principles and management methods common in the advanced sectors of Western industry. It would seem desirable—as part of a common Atlantic effort —to search for ways to motivate private industry to participate in the international effort. To illustrate what might be done, one private researcher[6] has proposed that as many NATO nations as possible impose a tax on industries relative to the pollution costs they inflict on the environment. This would create an incentive to invest in R & D on pollution control. The sharing of this knowledge might be accomplished by applying the pollution tax revenues to compensate firms for their R & D expenditures on pollution control, on condition that they make the technology readily available for wide dissemination (perhaps through NATO's CCMS).

The non-profit, non-governmental sector of Atlantic society would also have a good deal to contribute. There are various think tanks and futurist groups in most Atlantic countries, who are generally itching to give their ideas public airing.

There might be, for example, a sort of Atlantic clearinghouse to collect and analyze, with the aid of computers, and

[6]Joseph Harned, of Washington, D.C., in an unpublished paper.

then to disseminate suggested or proven solutions to the full range of environmental problems, including green belt conservation, town planning, leisure, population growth, urban transport, and so on. Much will depend on how comprehensively and efficiently a joint intelligence network of this sort could be made to function.

THE CIVIC DEVELOPMENT OF THE ATLANTIC SYSTEM

The new plans for improving the environment which we have described look at man's predicament largely in ecological perspective, *i.e.*, in terms of the relationship between life forms and their environment. But there is another group of problems of a different sort. These are the central issues surrounding the future of the Atlantic civic culture. They concern man's relationship to man, in the most profound sense. They require philosophical choices and value judgments. For example:

—the ends of education: human beings or packaged products for a technetronic age?

—possibilities for more participation, for decentralizing the nation-state's political institutions, for letting the individual and the small group make more of the decisions which vitally affect them;

—the rights and protection of minorities: ethnic, religious, cultural, racial, and other;

—the political responsibilities, rights, and privileges of young people;

—the conception of a new kind of civic education and programs of civic development, which might extend public comprehension of the values inherent in the Atlantic Idea and show how these can be applied to modern life;[7]

—the concept of public service, military, civilian, and voluntary.

[7]Educators were spurred by Sputnik in 1957 to conceive a "new math" and a "new physics" and schools have adopted the methods widely; but no one has yet effectively presented a "new civics."

Such questions go to the core of the West's political heart. In each case, one can discern a common need among the Atlantic countries to re-evaluate, re-establish, and renovate both values and institutions, to create fresh political conceptions to replace those no longer relevant, to restore the Atlantic civic culture.

How could one get at fundamental issues of this kind in a meaningful way?

One of the great political creations of the Atlantic system has been the British Royal Commission, emulated especially in other English-speaking countries. The work of these unusual bodies has served to attract broad public interest to crucial questions before society, and at the same time to insure that the political authorities would be seized with the correct issues and with the outlines of solutions. The same institutional approach might be employed on an Atlantic basis, involving youth along with adults, to deal with the more fundamental civic choices.

We quoted above from Article 2 of the North Atlantic Treaty. Another section of that Article states: "The Parties will contribute toward the further development of peaceful and friendly international relations by strengthening their free institutions, by bringing about a better understanding of the principles upon which these institutions are founded, and by promoting conditions of stability and well-being."

Real peace, NATO's goal, is far more than the absence of war. It depends upon removal of the root causes of wars, upon providing the individual with freedom, dignity, and opportunity.

There is considerable logic, as well as considerable difficulty, in the idea that NATO's members, having provided well for Atlantic security, should now train their sights on a humane, just, and prosperous Atlantic society.

CHAPTER 3

Gaps in the Future: The American Challenge and the European Challenge

"And quit fooling around with the Australia bit," said Jack Brody of Pasadena, Calif., as he tried to place a restaurant reservation with the man at the other end of the line. But Reg Bradshaw—at the other end—insisted that all HE was trying to do was to get a call through to an airline office in downtown Melbourne. Somehow, somewhere, a neurotic circuit had flipped out and connected Mr. Brody's call to Los Angeles with Mr. Bradshaw's local call from his home in a Melbourne suburb.[1]

INTERNATIONAL HERALD TRIBUNE,

Mr. Brody and Mr. Bradshaw, alas, are likely to hear more— not less—from one another over the coming years! The technological revolution has caught hold of us all. The Vatican, the Kremlin, and the urbanized West are all dealing with the pressures of technology on a rampage.

Among the ramifications of burgeoning technology are certain transatlantic phenomena known as "gaps."

Europeans began some years ago to talk about a "technological gap" between them and America. Upon inspection, it appeared that there might not be one, but several gaps,

[1] Paris, September 28, 1968.

including a "research gap," a "management gap," an "educational gap," and an "attitude gap." There may— or may not—be others. But if a large number of observers agree that there is some kind of gap, then there is at least a question to look into. Why are the gaps important? What are they? Are there any "reverse gaps" wherein the United States must catch up with Europe?

THE U. S. CLOUD ON EUROPE'S HORIZON

The editor and publisher of *L'Express* (France's *Time*-like magazine) is young, dynamic, Jean-Jacques Servan-Schreiber. In 1967 his book, *The American Challenge,*[2] astounded the European literary scene; in three months it sold half a million copies. Servan-Schreiber's thesis, which riveted so many Europeans to their armchairs, is this: the United States is far ahead of Europe in the practical application of technology. The gap, he says, is not narrowing but widening, especially in the "leading edge" industries of computers, airframes, and electronics. Unless counterbalanced, fears Servan-Schreiber, this U. S. superiority, especially in computers, "will lead eventually to permanent European industrial helotry." The third industrial power in the world, after America and Russia, will be not Europe but "U. S. industry in Europe."

There is little anti-Americanism in Servan-Schreiber's book; if anything, he is perhaps too sympathetic and understanding, for he says in effect to Europeans: "It's your own fault if you are behind. By comparison with the Americans, your management practices are outmoded, your education systems antiquated, your labor relations shocking, and your attitudes in general nineteenth century." His main antidote for these doldrums is to unite Europe into one state, with the combined mobilized resources, the scope, and scale for great creative enterprises which would enable it to meet "the American challenge."

[2] American edition published by Atheneum, New York, 1968.

We inspect some of the relevant economic statistics in Chapter Four of this book; Europe and America each has invested about the same amount in the other continent. But the American stake in Europe stirs up more controversy because the bulk of it is invested in direct control of businesses, while the Europeans are more content to buy stocks and bonds and receive the dividends and clip the coupons.

It is not the American share of ownership in European industry overall which concerns knowledgeable Europeans (around 5 per cent in most European countries, probably no more than 10 per cent in any of them[3]). Nor does U. S. investment constitute a predominant share in the total of all foreign investment in European industry.[4]

What does excite Europeans is the developing strategy of American industry overseas: it is concentrating on manufacture and largely on a few vital industries. Today, roughly one-fifth of all U. S. investment in manufacturing goes abroad, and the largest share of that to Europe. It was estimated that in 1966 the American electrical industry spent 19 per cent of its total investment in plant and equipment overseas, chemicals 28 per cent, rubber 30 per cent, and the transport equipment industry 27 per cent; this last was overwhelmingly investment in the European auto industry,[5]

Of the fourteen largest automobile companies in Europe, General Motors, Ford, and Chrysler are responsible for 30 per cent of the turnover. In petroleum, U. S.-owned companies had between 25 and 30 per cent of the market in the U. K. and the Common Market Six by 1964. In 1965, U. S. firms in Europe put 72 per cent of their new investments in plant and equipment into the key growth industries—

[3] Christopher Layton, in his study for the Atlantic Institute, *Trans-Atlantic Investments,* 1968 (pp. 13-14), quotes a number of recent analyses of U. S. investment abroad. One, by the German Bundesbank, concluded that the American share in the nominal capital of German public corporations in 1965 was about 5 per cent.
[4] For example, two-thirds of all foreign investment in West Germany in 1964 was held not by the U. S. but by other, mainly European, countries. Only in Britain, where U. S. ownership was 72 per cent of foreign investment in 1962, is the American share more than half of the total foreign investment.
[5] Layton, p. 17.

chemicals, transportation equipment, and electrical and non-electrical machinery. In short, *the main thrust of U. S. business in Europe is into the industries with new ideas, new processes, new applications, and new markets.*

In aerospace and electronics (including computers), U. S. firms have a particular advantage over European enterprises; massive U. S. Government spending for defense and space programs has biased the competitive position, giving American industry a commanding lead. Even though some aircraft firms in Europe (particularly British and French) are both large and technologically advanced, they are inexorably slipping back in the race with large American firms such as Boeing, Lockheed, and McDonnell-Douglas. The situation in the European computer market is dramatic; in 1964, an estimate of company shares in new installations showed IBM with 62 per cent of the total; its nearest competitor, International Computers Ltd. (a British firm), had 9 per cent and a handful of other firms, mostly European, divided up the rest in bits of one to seven per cent.[6]

Some Europeans complain not only about American penetration of their markets, but about American practices. American companies are criticized for laying off workers on purely economic grounds without considering social effects, or for not observing "fair commercial practices" long established in Europe. (Often this means that they decline to act in tacit restraint of trade with fellow manufacturers.) In European eyes, American firms pay their employees, especially managers, too much. They draw off many of the best people, notably scientists and engineers.

U. S. companies not only forge into European markets with large sums of dollars behind them, but they often—and increasingly—raise investment capital on the *European* market, competing with European firms for finance, and in

---

[6] Layton, Appendix, Table XVII. Brzezinski also ("America in the Technetronic Age," *Atlantic Community Quarterly*, Summer 1968, pp. 176–177) cites some telling statistics: 80 per cent of all scientific and technological discoveries of the last few decades originated in the United States; 75 percent of all the world's computers operate in the U. S. and the American lead in lasers is even more marked.

effect, invading Europe with Europe's own money. And U. S. corporations have been quicker than European firms to exploit the potential of the Common Market by establishing production and marketing branches EEC-wide. Investment by firms of the Six in each other's countries, although increasing, is surprisingly slight. One observer has commented, "It seems as if American capital will be the federalizer of European business and not the Common Market."[7]

Yet, despite the inconveniences, much of Europe genuinely wants American enterprise and more of it. European governments vie with one another to attract U. S. firms. The Belgian government gives grants of 30 per cent of the value of the investment to American companies settling there; the Dutch have upped the ante to 40 per cent. U. S. corporations, in effect, put themselves "up for auction among the competing European governments to make the best deal."[8] For the influx of American capital and skill benefits Europe, and governments and most businessmen know this; "it would be self-mutilation for Europe to deprive itself of the benefits by restrictive policies designed to keep American investment out."[9]

The central question therefore is not, "Is there too much or too little U. S. investment?" but, "Can Europe keep pace with America in new technologies and economic growth?" or, to put it another way, "Can Europe learn to use and benefit from U. S. investment without becoming subordinate?"

Finding the answer is neither simple nor easy.

THE AMERICAN CHALLENGE

Servan-Schreiber explains the significance of the new technologies:

[7] David P. Calleo, *Europe's Future: The Grand Alternatives* (New York: Horizon Press), 1965, p. 61.
[8] Servan-Schreiber, p. 16.
[9] Layton, p. 140.

We are in the process of compressing time and space in a way that was inconceivable ten years ago. Even more importantly, we are learning how to *intensify human experience* through centralized information and instant communication. This is a new world, one filled with adventure and risks.[10]

Modern power, he says,

is based on the capacity for innovation, which is research, and the capacity to transform inventions into finished products, which is technology. The wealth we seek does not lie in the earth or in numbers of men or machines, but in the human spirit. And particularly in the ability of man to think and create.[11]

America, says Servan-Schreiber, today resembles Europe "with a fifteen year head start." She is part of the same industrial society that began in the eighteenth century, but by 1980 she will have entered another world. If Europe fails to catch up, the United States "will have a monopoly on know-how, science, and power."[12]

Brzezinski calls the new era "the technetronic age," and defines it as "a society that is shaped culturally, psychologically, socially, and economically by the impact of technology and electronics, particularly computers and communications."[13] Computers, for both Servan-Schreiber and Brzezinski, play a central role in the new era because they are the means of extending man into whole new possibilities of life, just as steam power propelled him into the Industrial Age.

Given all this new power, a lonely America will become, for Servan-Schreiber, "the place where decisions are made."[14] In a single generation, he asserts, America will no longer belong to the same civilization.

From these conclusions, he forms one of his main recom-

[10] P. 89.
[11] P. 276.
[12] P. 101.
[13] Brzezinski, note 6, p. 175.
[14] Servan-Schreiber, p. 144.

mendations—a precondition for escaping American "colonization"—*i.e.,* that Europe collectively needs to become a great power, through political unification, so that the Americans will not have a monopoly on technological progress and thereby "lose the stimulation that comes from competition." Otherwise, the United States would have to work out new forms of social organization by itself and "would look on imperialism as a kind of duty."[15]

Servan-Schreiber is too balanced and objective, and too familiar with America, to advocate European withdrawal and protectionism in the face of this challenge; instead he calls on Europeans to unite. He says that mere "cooperative projects"—such as the British-French effort to build supersonic *Concorde*—will not do, because they are paralyzed by "the limitations of national diplomacy" and the doctrine of "fair shares," which insists that each country participating in a joint venture will receive a share of the contracts in strict proportion to its investment, regardless of economic efficiency. Cooperative projects are "only a caricature" of what is needed.

Servan-Schreiber conceives his European union vaguely, but it is clear that he advocates a true federation, exercising powers of its own, and in particular the power to fuse economies (contemplated but not yet accomplished by the Common Market), "capable of studying markets and resources, and then deciding where Europeans should concentrate their efforts." It would have to have authority in certain areas over the nation-states, and also its own financial resources, so that it could carry out large-scale projects across borders. It would have to be able to act by majority vote. It would subsidize "frontier" research and its applications, in the same way that the American government does today.

Servan-Schreiber acknowledges that a few European countries, notably Sweden, have been able to match American technology (at least in certain fields) and living standards without combining politically with other countries. The

[15] Pp. 102–103.

key to their achievement, he states, is that they have elected to *specialize;* they cannot match America over the broad spectrum of new industry. Although "rich in social potential," these small countries cannot be a model for Europe if she is to compete with the United States, for "Sweden has no ambitions to be a world power."[16] But France, Germany, and Britain—at least—do and therefore must unite.

Servan-Schreiber does not claim that political union alone would enable the Europeans to meet successfully the American challenge, but it would be the principal element, a sort of key: "By itself a political act can free aspirations trapped in confining, antiquated social structures."[17]

A REPLY TO SERVAN-SCHREIBER

It is easy to sympathize with the view that Europe cannot afford to slip behind the United States as it enters the new "technetronic age." One can also see that a European political union would probably help, particularly by focusing funds and central decision-making power on technological development. It might also "free aspirations" in a new chemical mix of federation, but here Servan-Schreiber sets foot on shakier ground. He is looking at this problem with European eyes—and French-European eyes at that. Seen from across the ocean or from a hypothetical epicenter high above the Atlantic system, we may get different answers, or at least some additional ones.

First, some American industrialists believe that in many sectors the Europeans are at least neck-and-neck with us and ahead in others. The Dutch have shown that it is not necessary to have a large, highly-protected home base in order to compete with the giants of international industry. Philips, the great Dutch electrical company, comes fifth worldwide, among the largest companies in its field. A merger by the main Dutch banks recently produced a bank-

16 P. 111.
17 P. 180.

ing group of world stature. The largest food company in the world—more than twice the size of its nearest rivals—is the Anglo-Dutch Unilever. In chemicals, the 1965 turnover of the nine largest European companies was about as large as the turnover of the nine largest American companies. Technologically, there is little difference in the modernity of the European compared with the American chemical industries. In basic steel, the United States is not competitive with Europe and Japan.

So the picture is not entirely one-sided. Confining national boundaries have not prevented some European firms from thinking and acting big, and others are learning fast. Therefore, although M. Servan-Schreiber has painted a generally faithful portrait of the "gap," another portraitist, from a different perspective and with a different light, might not achieve such a disturbing effect. If some European companies can "make it," why can't others?

A second question for M. Servan-Schreiber: Is European political union *the* answer which will suddenly free large numbers of Europeans from their industrial backwardness? Would it really strike at the roots of the difficulty? To the extent that a central authority would stimulate research, produce a common plan for leading-edge industries and subsidize their development—as the United States government does—political union could undoubtedly help, and might help a great deal. But although it cannot be proved, we nevertheless put forward the hypothesis that the most fundamental European obstacle to technological and business modernity lies in *social attitudes,* in the retarded pace of social change which fails to match industrial needs and possibilities.

The slow pace of social change is evident to be sure in America, but here the great lag has been in attitudes towards social, not economic, needs; in Europe the gap is in attitudes towards the forces of production and consumption. In both places the winds of change are now blowing.

In the United States there is an atmosphere which, far

more generally than in Europe, liberates the creative powers
and the initiative of the individual. It is likely, although
impossible to prove, that the persistence of such European
attitudes is a much deeper source of that continent's in-
capacity to compete with American technology and business than is Europe's political disunity or the fragmentation
of her markets. The advanced positions of a few small countries, where there is more scope for initiative, suggest however that this may be the case. The federation of Europe may
prove disappointing if Servan-Schreiber and others expect
that it will cure a deeply-entrenched structural backwardness in much of European society.

Our third riposte to M. Servan-Schreiber is this: Are you
really sure that you want for Europe all that the United
States has, and is getting, from the mix of advanced technology and modern business? We Americans are a dynamic
people, we have learned how to liberate human imagination
and drive so that we can make more things and make more
things work better, we are clearly in the forefront of world
technology, we have the world's greatest corporations, we
have the highest standard of living, we have the largest GNP
and (still) the most gold. But . . . in some ways, different from
your own, M. Servan-Schreiber, we too are backward. The
incidence of poverty in the American population may be
greater than in any west European country north of the Alps
and the Pyrenees, although this is difficult to prove because
of variations in statistics and criteria. Our rate of unemployment is higher than that in any of the Scandinavian or Common Market countries[18] or Great Britain. Medical services
are more widely available to the whole population in almost any northwestern European country than in America.
Our illiteracy rate is higher than are Britain's, West Germany's, Holland's, or Scandinavia's. Our crime rates are also
higher. The incidence of mental disease and the prevalence
of psychiatric treatment are higher. And our ability—
or perhaps our will—to control inflation lags significantly

[18] Except perhaps Italy's.

behind that of many European nations.

Most Americans would not live anywhere else on earth, and they may be justified. Most of the time-worn clichés about America are still true: it *is* the land of opportunity, it *is* (by comparison with others) the classless society, it *is* the citadel of constitutionalism and of freedom and democracy, of the Atlantic Idea. And, in America's defense, it has acute problems of race and ethnic assimilation far beyond those faced by any other Atlantic country. But there is nevertheless a great deal of unfinished business in America to make her practices square with her professed ideals, and the advent of the technetronic age so far is making the effort to close *this* gap more, not less, difficult.

Robert L. Heilbroner, in reviewing Servan-Schreiber's book, observed that the extension of American economic hegemony, "this tremendous and perhaps unmanageable thrust toward an American imperialism," is the real problem arising from the book. "Expansion with dogma, growth without plan, the extension of power without an extension of responsibility are the consequences of the ferocious dynamism of the American corporate system. . . . In the end the American challenge is that of a society caught in the grip of a momentum over which there exists no adequate social control."[19] Harsh words, and only one side of the coin, yet a side we must come back to before we phrase a final reply to M. Servan-Schreiber. For there may well be a "reverse gap" and a European challenge.

WHAT ARE THE "AMERICAN CHALLENGE" GAPS?

Let us try to define more precisely the gaps which Servan-Schreiber and others have discerned between the "advanced" Americans and the "backward" Europeans. There is first . . .

The research gap. In 1962 Europe spent 6 billion dollars on research and development compared with 16 billion dol-

[19] *Saturday Review*, August 10, 1968, p. 24.

lars by the United States. In 1964 the United States spent 3 per cent of its national income on research, Europe 2 per cent.[20] This gap exists partly because the U. S. Government spends more for this purpose than all the European governments put together, and partly because of more extravagant private U. S. outlays for salaries and equipment at inflated price levels. But mainly the gap is a reflection of the lesser importance which European industry places on research.

The research gap however is less important than others. An Atlantic Institute conference paper in 1968 asserted that the basic technological disparities between Europe and America are not of knowledge but "rest in the differences in value systems and attitudes, managerial practices, institutions, capital availabilities, and priorities among nations and among regions."[21] Among the key elements singled out at the Conference for improvement were the educational systems of the European countries, whose shortcomings underlie most of the other "gaps."

The education gap between Europe and America, in many respects, is great. In a recent year the U. S. had four times as many college graduates as the six Common Market countries. (Total populations are about equal.) In the United States, three to five times as many children of workers and farmers have access to higher education as in the EEC countries.[22] At the same time, there were more than three times as many American university graduates in science as there were in the Common Market countries, which must obviously have some relevance to the gap in technology.[23]

In a report for the OECD, Professor Joseph Ben-David

---

[20] Layton, note 3, p. 94.

[21] Report of Conference on *Strategies for Atlantic Technological Development* (Paris: The Atlantic Institute), 1968.

[22] It is curious that even though in most of Europe there are few financial obstacles to the most talented students, regardless of social origins, because of the availability of government scholarships, the children of workers and peasants *generally do not apply for them*. Thus, age-old social attitudes persist when there is no longer an economic basis for them.

[23] Servan-Schreiber (note 2, p. 74) quotes these figures from recent studies by E. F. Denison and Raymond Poignant.

explored some of the ways in which European university obsolescence contributes to the persistence of a gap with America. Part of the difficulty, he found, is in the structure of European universities, which is unduly cumbersome and antiquated. "The result," says Ben-David, "has been that the science organizations of the different European countries have become increasingly unable to take full advantage of new ideas, even when these were initiated in the same countries." Ideas, and often the researchers themselves, have usually had to migrate to the United States "in order to be rid of the various kinds of interference due to the obsolescence and poverty of the different local systems." [24]

Europe so far has not been able or willing to modify its fundamentally elitist ideas about secondary and higher education, to put the necessary resources into education, to streamline academic structures, to make education serve modern society.

Then there is *the management gap*. "What threatens to crush us today" says Servan-Schreiber, "is not a torrent of riches, but a more intelligent use of skills."[25] American management is more flexible than European and organizes itself better. American management is used to organizing and planning on a continental basis, in contrast to European management. American management gets more out of its workers and executives. American management gets and pays for the best legal advice; the average U. S. firm in the Common Market will hire lawyers in every one of the six countries if necessary.

American management has been enormously improved in

[24] *Fundamental Research and the Universities* (Paris: OECD), 1968, pp. 87–88.
[25] P. 29. By way of illustration, Servan-Schreiber puts his finger on one of the key differences in American vs. European management practices. He discusses what he calls "the committee-boss relationship." The ideal (and the usual American) way, says Servan-Schreiber, is that while the choice of an industrial objective may well come out of a committee or board, "there can be only a single authority once the objective has been decided upon. This 'boss' is responsible for the entire operation, however large it may be, and must have considerable freedom of action and decision-making power." (p. 168.) This is not the usual practice in a European firm, one reason why American management is thought to be more flexible.

the past three or four decades through the rise of powerful schools of business management in leading universities, which turn out better-equipped young managers than Europe's and which also provide American industry with a wealth of research and information directly pertinent to the tasks of management. "Technological innovation," said the London *Economist* recently, "requires a certain state of mind and the Americans have it because they employ better-educated managers."[26] Business management schools are growing in Europe, but not nearly fast enough. French industry traditionally will still recruit a majority of its young executives from the discipline of academic economics, and British firms will still take most of theirs from among young men who have "done" undergraduate classics or history or sociology at Oxford, Cambridge or a red-brick university, or no university.

Although there are important exceptions to these generalizations (and in particular one should note the outstanding quality of management in some of the largest European firms), in its broad outlines this is an accurate picture.

If one asks "*Why* is European management so far behind?" the answers get even more complicated and murky. A European-turned-American businessman, Antonie T. Knoppers, says, "It is management attitude which has to pave the way for effective European technological development."[27]

Perhaps then we can also speak properly of an *attitude gap.* Not only the attitudes of managers are important, but those of scientists, engineers, civil servants, politicians, teachers—in fact anyone in Europe who has anything to do with the workings of the economy, including the consuming public. Social attitudes are influenced by a thousand subtle cultural and historical pressures, by traditions, by stories at

[26] "The Technological Gap," reprinted in the *Atlantic Community Quarterly,* Summer 1968, p. 190.
[27] In Gene Bradley (ed) *Building the European-American Market,* Homewood, Ill.: Dow Jones Irwin, 1967, p. 40.

mother's knee.[28] One theory is that the most enterprising, adventurous, individualistic people left Europe, bound for the New World and other colonies, because they couldn't abide the tight mold of European society. In any event, America developed in a freer, easier atmosphere and, mindlessly, American society picked and chose among the European social strains it would cultivate or discard. The Europeans today are left with the full weight of an ancient heritage—proud, ennobling, cultivated, satisfying, enduring —but not in every respect attuned to the needs of the late-industrial and technetronic eras. (One wag has said that the Europeans are having less difficulty adjusting to the era of the Common Market than to that of the *super*market, which demands changes in consuming habits, archaic methods of food distribution, etc.)

Servan-Schreiber quotes Michel Crozier:

Thus our problems are rooted in the need to change the hopelessly ossified European societies which find it so difficult to become more flexible.

The existence of this attitude gap, reflected in management, education, research, and technological gaps, is one of contemporary Europe's greatest problems. Essentially, the existence of the full range of gaps means that human assets are used inadequately, wastefully.

WAYS TO CLOSE THE "AMERICAN CHALLENGE" GAPS

Numerous suggestions have been made for measures which Europeans or Americans, or both, could take in order to deal with the various gaps effectively. The reader may be interested in a few samples.

[28] David Frost, a BBC Television interlocutor, recently interviewed San Francisco's waterfront philosopher Eric Hoffer. "What do you believe is the basic difficulty with the British economy?" he asked. Hoffer answered, "I think every Englishman deep down wants to be a country squire. . . . Well, they can't *all* be country squires; someone's got to do the work."

Education

1. Europe should invest more in the renovation and expansion of teaching, professional training, and research and, for those already in industry, adult education. James Perkins has said, "Until this reform is completed, the European educational system will be the bottleneck that shuts off the development of Europe's manpower and shortens the life of its great dreams."[29]

2. Various proposals have been made, beginning more than a decade ago, for a major new university of science and technology, an all-European "M.I.T." One government or another—often the French—has balked. A major sticking point has always been finance; European countries, hard-pressed to finance domestic universities, are reluctant to take on external obligations.

3. More European management training schools are an urgent need, but there is a severe shortage both of public funds to set them up and qualified personnel to teach. Finance might come from small and medium-sized European businesses, which need trained managers, and from U. S. firms in Europe. Some American business schools might set up branches in Europe—not primarily for their own students, but for Europeans. (In a more general field, that of American Studies, the Salzburg Seminar, a U. S. institution for Europeans originated by a group from Harvard University, has demonstrated the feasibility of such schemes.)

Research and Development

4. American firms in Europe, perhaps stimulated by tax incentives, could establish more of their own research and development (R & D) centers in Europe, to train European research personnel, engender emulation and competition, and stimulate social mobility. There ap-

[29]Quoted by John Diebold in "Is the Gap Technological?" *Foreign Affairs*, January 1968.

pears to be a special need for applying R & D to the production of marketable goods and services.

5. An overall strategy for European science and technology could be developed by a common authority, with power to plan and support R & D on a European scale; to finance independently of national governments all-European projects in the frontier technologies; to harmonize existing patent and licensing procedures; to support multinational training programs; and to coordinate the various national requirements and programs in the new industries. There has been press speculation about a "European Technological Community," one of Servan-Schreiber's proposals, but so far no apparent initiatives.

6. European astronauts were not included in the Apollo moon program, but perhaps the first Mars flight could be made an Atlantic, not just an American, venture. Two embryonic European efforts at space cooperation, ELDO and ESRO,[30] enfeebled by national restrictions and hesitations, are moving slowly. Could not the U. S. National Aeronautics and Space Administration (NASA) help to preserve a common European framework by subcontracting one of its major space projects to its transatlantic partners? NASA's offers to cooperate in major ways with Russian space programs have made front-page headlines.

7. All Atlantic countries share major problems of environmental pollution; a multinational corporation might be formed to study and attack some of these problems on a demonstration-pilot basis.

Investment

8. Recently the Federal and some state governments, plus bodies such as the National Association of Manufacturers, have been encouraging more European direct in-

---

[30] The European Launcher Development Organization and the European Space Research Organization.

vestment in the United States. Olivetti, which bought Underwood Typewriters, is one of several European firms which have recently taken the plunge. The French Pechiney (aluminum), the Belgian Saint Gobin (glass), and the German BASF (chemicals) are others. Among the many obstacles to European investment in America, finance is usually a major one; perhaps European corporations could emulate American investors and raise a big part of the capital for U. S. ventures *in the U. S. capital market*. This might bolster European pride and provide one more vehicle for that thorough mixing-up of the Atlantic economies which alone, in the end, will insure that all the gaps are closed. The United States would doubtless benefit from technical and other skills which European-directed firms could introduce through their American subsidiaries. The U. S. Government recently relaxed tax provisions to attract European direct investment; perhaps more incentives should be offered.

9.   The weak, fragmented capital markets of Europe should be tied together more effectively, putting European firms who seek credit for expansion on the same footing as their U. S. rivals. The astounding development of the Eurodollar demonstrates both the need and the possibilities for an Atlantic-wide money market.

This short catalogue of ameliorative measures is meant only to be illustrative. Finding ways and means is mainly a European problem but the United States could do a good deal to help.

Probably the most effective way to dissolve any of these gaps—and particularly the "attitude gap"—is to encourage much more intra-Atlantic migration, short-term and long-term, of the movers and shakers of the economies:

More educational exchanges.

More joint training establishments.

More sabbaticals for travel and study abroad.

More multinational conferences.

More periods of work abroad, including temporary job-swapping, or periods of "looking over the shoulder" of one's counterparts in other countries.

The best locus for efforts to narrow the "American Challenge" gaps is with leadership, the human key to motivation, renovation, cooperation, and forward movement.

But to rest content with having discussed some possible causes and cures for European "backwardness" would be to have looked at but half the picture. Not only is the forward movement of the European branch of Atlantic civilization at stake, but the quality of the other part, the American branch, also.

THE EUROPEAN CHALLENGE

Can one say that because the American economy is more "advanced," U. S. management attitudes are necessarily superior?

For there is a "European Challenge" to America, as well as an American Challenge to Europe.

Who has not met the American, returned from a sojourn in Europe, who yearns for a more civilized tempo, a more tranquil and pleasing environment, more sensitivity and style, better commuter transport, *Gemütlichkeit*, art in daily life, and whole towns that are like parks? Who would welcome in his American life more intimacy in conversation, architecture, and literature; more feminine, mysterious women; more grace, cultivation, forethought, contemplation, time? Who has suddenly begun to realize that in practically every department of modern urban life, outside of work, one European people or another has come up with better solutions than the people of the United States and applied the solutions more broadly and evenly?

Yet what American has not met the European, perhaps partly educated in the United States, who longs to introduce American methods in his business, or his schools, or his local community; to enshrine efficiency and give stale tradition a back seat; to shake up his stuffy colleagues, their organizations, and "the system"; to place a bet on the individual?

In part, the social crisis of Western civilization is that Americans have some of the answers to Man's attempt to cope with headlong change, that Europeans have another set of answers, but that *both* sets are needed. Americans need European inspiration and the European model to help them give more quality to life by closing the American "satisfaction gaps": the landscape, free time, amenities, taste, fine arts, conservation, poverty, social care, public transport, and urban environment gaps. Europeans need Americans—literally—to infuse them with dynamism, to stimulate enterprise, to dissolve the bonds of class, to displace cynicism with good will and confidence, to update and democratize education, to apply the fruits of inquiry in more practical ways, to substitute an expansive for a restrictive view of human beings.

Europeans and Americans need one another.

There are dangers.

What if Europe, in seeking to emulate American technology, gains technetronic parity but loses its soul by putting the capstone on the de-humanized consumer society towards which the predominant forces of the age are pushing us?

What if Americans cannot be sufficiently humble about their shortcomings to look for help? What if they fail to recognize that Europe's aspirations to follow America into the post-industrial era are legitimate, and that we must help to get her there, along with ourselves? The validity and the wholeness of Western civilization are at stake.

One of the more favorable omens for the future is the evidence, in both Europe and North America, of willingness to work together in identifying and solving common problems. The Atlantic Institute headquartered in Paris has undertaken an extensive series of studies and conferences on these subjects, the results of which form part of the basis for this chapter.

SUMMING UP

Important "gaps" exist—on both sides—between Europe and America.

The culture of the modern American economy, for all its dynamism, has had unfortunate side effects. In pursuing industrial and financial growth and power, the United States has to some extent neglected the quality of its life, the impact of technological change on the urban environment, and important social ills. There is an American "attitude gap." In these areas, Europe has much experience and wisdom upon which the United States could draw.

Europe is behind the United States in energizing, managing, and exploiting its economy. It spends too little on research and far too little on the practical applications of research. Its educational systems generally require updating. Although many changes have occurred in Europe's stultified social patterns, old ways in most countries still hamper dynamic movement. The attitudes of Europeans bound up with the economy, from entrepreneurs down to consumers, are in many ways unsuited to realizing the full potential of the new technetronic age on our horizons. There is considerable danger that Europe will remain largely behind while America enters this future alone, and that American business in time will dominate Europe. It is also possible that Europe will instead seek economic isolation in an attempt, which would probably prove vain, to attain parity.

The most rational vision of the future encompasses one intercontinental Atlantic economy, employing all productive resources irrespective of national boundaries.

Defining the problem and the solutions in this way presents to youth on both sides of the ocean a challenge which should stir their imagination and their loyalty. It cries aloud for their participation. It relates at every phase to the practical affairs of daily life. It makes an idealistic appeal to humanitarian motives, if explained and understood.

PART II

The Atlantic Economy

If the emergence of an interdependent Atlantic society has become discernable, the existence of an Atlantic economy is many times more apparent. The internal political pressures of States and the uncertainties and false hopes connected with the seemingly endless Cold War probably have, on balance, a centrifugal effect on the Atlantic system. But since the end of World War II countless threads of commercial, financial, and industrial interests have been woven back and forth across and around the Atlantic to fashion an economic tapestry of surprising strength and durability.

For increasing numbers of business enterprises, the question now is not "Should we set up shop abroad?" Men of finance and industry in Europe, Canada, the United States, and Japan too are becoming increasingly impatient with the confining economic nation-states.

The next four chapters seek to portray the complexities

and frustrations as well as the opportunities inherent in the burgeoning of the Atlantic economy, the core of a world-wide economic community.

How can this vast mechanism be guided to steady, unencumbered, well-articulated growth? Is the international money system adequately developed to withstand the strains inherent in the move toward a single intercontinental economy? Can we and should we go all the way to free trade? In all of this, how can the Atlantic community find satisfactory relations with the less developed countries?

CHAPTER 4

Managing the Atlantic Economy

As the mobility of goods, services, capital, business enterprise, technology, and labor increase, divergent national objectives will be increasingly difficult to achieve and national
autonomy increasingly threatened. In the face of high international mobility, the nation-state—admittedly a very dura-
ble form of political organization— becomes outmoded in
the realm of economic policy, at least under the rules and
conventions of international behavior that the major industrial countries have adopted. [1]

RICHARD N. COOPER

Since World War II, the economies of the Atlantic system
have matured remarkably. Whereas before there were fierce
debates as to what constituted a "good" economic regime,
what justified state intervention in the economy, what
caused depressions, what brought prosperity, and so on, in
recent years the economic systems of western Europe and
North America have quietly begun to align themselves, sort-
ing out the relevance of economic theory to practice, forming a broad consensus on the main questions of public policy,
and at the same time growing together into one vast area for

[1] *Ventures,* New Haven.

production, trade, and consumption. H. van B. Cleveland has characterized this new Atlantic economic system succinctly:

There has been a marked convergence of national economic regimes and policies toward a norm which although it may be called "socialism" in Western Europe and "capitalism" in America, is in fact a mixed system whose spirit is pragmatic and unideological. The relevant features of this system are a commitment to high employment and rapid growth with minimal inflation; control of the general conjuncture by fiscal and monetary policy, private ownership and control of business, apart from public utilities and, in Europe, some nationalized industries which on the whole behave much as privately-owned companies do; detailed market control by public authorities in agriculture but stress on competition as the principal regulator in the rest of the economy.[2]

The maturing of this system has meant that each Atlantic country has been able to act in economic affairs with more confidence; this in turn has begun to open the way for each to interact with the others in the interest of international economic balance. A better understanding of how the international economy works, and a greater readiness to apply this knowledge have now permeated the consciousness of political leaders, economists, bankers, and industrialists. National governments are being forced more and more to take into account economic indicators and developments elsewhere. The idea of a series of separate, more or less watertight national economic units today is slowly receding; those with their hands on the levers are learning that the Atlantic countries have no choice but to make economic interdependence work.

This new approach towards a Western consensus on objectives and methods of economic management does not mean we have mastered the governance of affairs, so as to

[2] *The Atlantic Idea and Its European Rivals,* New York: McGraw-Hill, for the Council on Foreign Relations), 1966, p. 156.

assure continuous prosperity and full employment. Far from it; adjustments and recessions still occur. But it does mean that the path ahead is gradually being cleared of many narrowly nationalistic notions and practices. Thus the way is being opened for new ideas and new organizations.

THE COMMON MARKET AND THE EUROPEAN FREE TRADE ASSOCIATION

The most dramatic symbol of the new economic approach is the Common Market—the European Economic Community. The intent of those who created the European Economic Community and its two adjuncts, the Coal and Steel and Atomic Energy Communities, was to fuse the economies of the six participants, make war among them impossible and political union among them more likely. The United States sympathized fully and actively. While the United States Government deplored the trade discrimination involved, which could hurt other countries, the continuous official position has been that the achievement of the political purposes and the long-run economic advantages would justify the temporary economic inconveniences.

Economically, the three European Communities have been an overall success. In the first ten years, trade among EEC members increased more than 250 per cent; world trade in the same period expanded by only 89 per cent. Living standards of their peoples have improved markedly. Labor now moves relatively freely among the Six. The customs union, eliminating all tariffs and quotas on industrial goods traded within the Common Market and imposing a single tariff on all goods imported from outside, went into effect eighteen months ahead of schedule, on July 1, 1968.

Industrialists in the Six have found it easier to adjust to this freedom of trade than they had feared, but have been slow to take full advantage of the Market by crossing national frontiers to merge their firms into multinational corporations. While a number of "Europe-wide" businesses and the beginnings of a Continental money market, based on "Euro-dollars," have developed, it is largely American companies and banks which have led the way, which have best understood the potential and been quickest to seize initiative.

A customs union was only intended as a first step towards full economic union of the Six. But beyond the domain of trade, most of the tough problems, such as a unified transport policy, a common currency, the harmonization of taxes and patent legislation, remain largely unsolved. Both European firms and governments have shown timidity in "thinking big" about the Common Market. Sometimes governments (the French in the 1968 Fiat-Citroën Case) have blocked transnational business mergers for national reasons. Nevertheless, the EEC has on balance unquestionably stimulated economic growth and prosperity among its members.

The effect of the Common Market on outside countries has been less salubrious. It has certainly discriminated in trade against the other countries of western Europe, seven of whom in 1960 formed the European Free Trade Association[3] to lessen the impact and put pressure on the EEC for an accommodation. Among themselves, the EFTA countries achieved free trade even before the Common Market, and the amount of increased trade among them has almost equaled the high EEC levels.

But the split of Europe into two competing trading camps has satisfied no one and stands in the way of further economic progress. To heal this breach, some EFTA members —notably Britain, Denmark, and Norway—seek full Common Market membership; others wish to be associates. With the change of government in France, negotiations have begun towards what may be in effect a merger of the two trading units.

---

[3] EFTA members are Britain, Denmark, Austria, Norway, Portugal, Sweden, and Switzerland. Finland is an associate. EFTA's free trade provisions have been limited to industrial products.

The trading power and the attractive idea of the new EEC accomplished more than good intentions and mild interest in trade liberalization had been able to do: it persuaded the U. S. Congress to adopt the liberal Trade Expansion Act of 1962. The United States feared that it would be hurt by the EEC, particularly in agricultural exports to Europe; this and threats of new barriers against many industrial products, together with the long-term advantages of wider markets and the freer flow of goods, convinced the Administration and Congress that sweeping action was needed. The result was the Kennedy Round, three years of international negotiations which cut tariffs between industrial countries by an average of about 35 per cent and averted, for the time being, what might have been a nasty trade war.

Protectionist forces are still strong, however, on both sides of the Atlantic. There is a growing tendency among some sections of American industry which suffer from European competition to ask, "Are the long-run advantages of European integration worth our immediate sacrifices?" In particular, the agricultural policy of the EEC raises continual problems for the United States and many other countries.

The high level of EEC agricultural levies was set up largely to satisfy the French, whose farm prices were higher than those of the other five members. The Germans have been less vocal in their demands, but their even less efficient agriculture has also benefited. Increases in EEC barriers to agricultural products have provoked countervailing duties from the United Kingdom, New Zealand, the United States, and others. With the present food price levels inside the Common Market, the other Four feel that they are subsidizing French and German agriculture.[4] There are some indica-

---

[4] It is easy to criticize the Common Market's agricultural policies, but these are actually little worse than those of most of the other industrialized countries. All of them are reacting to a common agricultural pressure, none of them in a far-sighted way. The EEC poses an acute problem primarily because of its new weight, as a unit, in the Atlantic and world agricultural scheme.

tions however that the skyrocketing cost of these subsidies may force a change in EEC policies.

In 1969, the devaluation of the franc and revaluation of the mark subjected the common agricultural policy to new strains. The attempt to incorporate Britain into the Common Market will bring still greater pressures, not least of all in the field of food policy.

On the positive side, the Common Market has stimulated growing American investment inside the Six. This is not only good for American business, but also has tended to strengthen the EEC, as most American firms operate throughout the Common Market. Hence, the United States has a strong economic as well as well as political interest in preserving and promoting European integration.

The Common Market's propensity to make treaties of association with large numbers of European and African countries, many of whom obviously cannot or do not wish ever to become full members, represents a danger to principles of trade liberalization and nondiscrimination, which characterize the Atlantic economic system. If Britain eventually were to join the Common Market, adding all or most of the Commonwealth to the existing scheme of EEC preferences, the resulting system would, without some counterbalancing action, hurt the United States, Japan, and other trading countries remaining outside. There is therefore a strong argument for preventing any further division of the Atlantic system into trading blocs, and for continuing the march towards freer trade on as broad a basis as possible.

To summarize: On balance the Common Market has been a most heartening development for the Atlantic system, for it has improved long-run chances for peace in Europe, greatly strengthened the economies of its members, and forced the issue of greater trade liberalization. EFTA too has made an important contribution.

On the negative side, the EEC's continued exclusion of Britain and other European countries who want to join has had some hurtful economic consequences and could have more. Although the EEC made heavy cuts in its common external tariff in the Kennedy Round, as did the United States, there is still danger that its trade policies will look more inward than outward, particularly in agriculture. Nevertheless, as a pace-setting model for wider integration and as the potential nucleus of a much larger trading area without barriers, the Common Market's emergence marks an imaginative, valuable forward step for the entire Atlantic system.

THE INTERNATIONAL BUSINESS COMMUNITY

Due to the acceleration of technology, the advent of the EEC, the recent movement towards freer trade, and other causes, the world of economic forces is being changed almost beyond recognition. Goods and managerial personnel now move quickly about the world. Developments in communication make it feasible to control far-flung decentralized production, marketing, and financial operations from a distant headquarters. Automated assembly lines and computers mean that tremendous savings in labor can be achieved, making it possible to manufacture hitherto expensive products for mass markets, or to plan intricate schemes, previously unrealizable (or even unplannable), for producing goods or rendering services in widely-scattered locations. General rises in living standards—within the Atlantic system, phenomenal rises—are now providing an enormous Atlantic market and the rudiments of similar markets in other regions of the world.

Demand, in the last analysis, governs an economy. Economist Peter Drucker lays his finger on the worldwide "community of information" which has created a "global shopping center," a single economy in its wants and expectations. And it is predominantly the industrialized nations of the Atlantic community who are producers, as well as consumers, for this "global shopping center."[5]

Because all these new factors are operating, a revolution in economic activity is taking place.

Whereas formerly competitive advantages for producers were mainly dependent on the nearness of raw materials, power, and other strictly geographic factors, today competitive advantage is more and more a question of how successfully an industrialist with an idea, a team of expert managers and technicians, and the right organizational patterns can transfer these components to a distant environment where there is a reasonably good supply of workmen and consumers. It is increasingly true, and particularly within the new transatlantic market, that the long-run cost of moving these conceptual and managerial elements in the production process to the market is lower than the cost of transporting merchandise for long distances from a central plant. This point is made by economist Emile Benoit, who says that companies which today provide such services "completely transcend the competitive-market assumptions of classical economists . . . "[6] As a result, a vast transatlantic movement of capital, managerial talent, and technical know-how is taking place, and manufacturing operations are being geographically dispersed, to an extent unknown in history.

American business has been quick to exploit these new possibilities. The advent of the Common Market, demolishing old walls to commerce, made the heart of Europe especially attractive. American investment there has increased on an almost geometric curve in the sixties.

By 1964, the sales of U. S. manufacturing subsidiaries in western Europe had reached $16.5 billion annually, almost four times the total of U. S. exports to Europe in that year, and sales of the subsidiaries were rising at a faster rate than exports.[7] These figures prompted William Diebold

[5] *The Age of Discontinuity* (New York: Harper and Row), 1969, pp. 80–81.

[6] *Disarmament and World Economic Interdependence* (New York: Columbia University Press), 1967. An extract, from which the above quote is taken, appears in the *Atlantic Community Quarterly*, Spring 1968, pp. 80–94.

[7] Bela Balassa, *Trade Liberalization Among Industrial Countries: Objectives and Alternatives* (New York: McGraw-Hill, for the Council on Foreign Relations), 1967,

of the Council on Foreign Relations to ask: "What is the American economy? Clearly it is not just a geographic entity surrounded by a tariff and an invisible monetary line."[8] The same could increasingly be said of European business, or even of the Canadian economy, which extends to a surprising extent south of the undefended border.

Economist Judd Polk has estimated that a U. S. investment abroad of some $60 billion produced an output of about $120 billion.[9] This figure was larger than the gross national product of any nation except the United States.

U. S. direct investment—book value—in Europe increased from $1.7 billion in 1950 to $17.8 billion in 1967. In the same period, European direct investment in the United States, starting from a higher level, increased from $2.2 billion to only $7 billion. Portfolio investment (minority purchases of stocks and bonds, which do not involve control) is a different matter; here U. S. ownership of European securities is far exceeded by European ownership of U. S. securities as shown below:

	U. S. Long-Term Investment in Western Europe	*Western Europe's Long-Term Investment in the U. S.*
	(End of 1967, in millions of dollars)	
Direct	17,882	7,004
Foreign dollar bonds	718	—
Corporate and Municipal bonds	—	1,440
Corporate securities	2,148	10,512
Other	966	1,291
Total	21,714	20,247

p. 131. These figures were based on a 1965 Department of Commerce Study, which has not been repeated.

[8] *Foreign Affairs*, January 1967, p. 297.

[9] Cited by Sidney Rolfe in *The Multinational Corporation in the World Economy: Direct Investment in Perspective* (New York: Praeger, for the Atlantic Council of the United States), 1970.

Considered together, all forms, including portfolio and direct, of European investment in the U. S. and of U. S. investment in Europe have come close to balancing.

It is evident that "whereas Europeans continue to salt away capital and savings in American corporations, American management has been bringing its ideas, techniques, and processes to Europe in the form of plant and factories. While European investors in the United States are often sleeping partners, the new American direct investors in Europe play an active evident part in the industrial life of Europe."[10]

Not only has American direct investment in Europe increased dramatically in recent years, but U. S. funds are being diverted from other areas of the world. "At the end of 1960, only one-fifth of U. S. direct investments were in Europe, and the European total was 20 per cent less than in Latin America and 70 per cent less than in Canada. By the end of 1967, direct investment in Europe had risen to 30 per cent of all private direct investments abroad, and the European total had become 50 per cent larger than investments in Latin America and about equal to those in Canada.[11]

The international Atlantic business community has been growing apace in the last decade, but the most dynamic growth has been that of American industry in western Europe. This, plus the fact that much of the American direct investment has been in the new technologies—computers, airframes, electronics, and oil—has given rise to questions as to the effects on United States-European relations. Clearly, if present trends are projected for some years ahead, it is entirely possible that the second industrial power in the world, after the United states, will become, as Jean-Jacques Servan-Schreiber has suggested, American business in Europe.

[10] Frederick A. Christopher Layton, *Trans-Atlantic Investments* (2nd ed.) (Paris: The Atlantic Institute), 1968, pp. 21–22.
[11] U. S. Department of Commerce, *Survey of Current Business,* October, 1968, p. 21.

The influx to western Europe of American private capital has, in many ways, simply continued the earlier stimulus of the Marshall Plan, providing capital for bold new ventures, underwriting rapid economic growth, and generally helping to raise wage levels, living standards, and returns on investment. Along with the influx of U. S. capital have come American managers, engineers, and their "know-how." Finally, there is the sizeable addition of so-called "Eurodollars," U. S. dollars which find their way overseas to European capital markets, are freely traded, and constitute the beginnings of a unified financial system for the Continent.

Despite these obvious advantages, European sensitiveness to the American presence can be readily understood, especially insofar as Europeans recognize that they must rely on the American nuclear deterrent for their ultimate defense. In discussing this question of dependence, Servan-Schreiber comes to the logical conclusion that the wise course for Europeans is to take full advantage of the influx of American investment and American management methods, and build their own economy into a competitive position by the use of the same tools. In this situation a duty also devolves on the overseas American corporation to be a good citizen of the country in which it finds itself. Most of them recognize that this is in their own self-interest.

If Europeans do not seize initiative, and if Americans do not use restraint, then in time Europe's economy may indeed come under virtual domination of the mother's big child on the western shores of the Atlantic.

BUSINESS LEAPS THE NATIONAL BARRIERS

Meanwhile, with few people thinking about such long-range issues, how does intercontinental Atlantic business manage? Corporate life is undergoing big changes.

Some theorists distinguish between an "international corporation" and a "multinational" one; the former is a company based in one country which nevertheless conducts manufacturing or other primary business operations in other countries. Most of the profits, sooner or later, flow "home" and the operations are controlled from "home." The multinational company, again according to these theorists, does not truly have a one-nation locus of operations. Its activities are spread over a number of countries, the nationals of several countries play leading roles in its management, and it is impossible to say that its ownership is concentrated in any single nation.[12]

By these standards, Royal Dutch Shell and Unilever, the great chemical, food, and soap company, are practically the only important examples of multinational corporations today. Both are controlled about equally by British and Dutch owners and managers and their senior staffs include significant numbers of other countries' nationals. The International Telephone and Telegraph Company has also gone a long way towards true multinationality.

Practically all the other giants of international business have their headquarters in one particular country and draw their main leadership from it. Yet there are different degrees of multinationality, and the trend is in the direction of more multinationality.

For many years strictly business considerations have led nearly all companies operating abroad to utilize maximum numbers of nationals of the host countries at lower management levels and to advance them when they were considered qualified. Today, most international companies have few "home-country" nationals based in other countries. Some, like Eastman Kodak, have none of their own nationals even in top management abroad.

Internationalization of home offices has proceeded more slowly. Many corporations, however, are now exchanging technical, middle, and "upper-middle" management personnel between home and overseas offices, regardless of na-

---

[12] A recent study indicates that more than four-fifths of the top 200 largest American enterprises, and two-thirds of the top 200 of all the other industrialized countries, are properly classed as international firms. See Gene Bradley (ed.), *Building the European-American Market* (Homewood, Ill.: Dow-Jones Irwin), 1967, p.23.

tionality. In a few rare cases, the very top executive positions in international companies are held by persons of other nationalities: the president of IBM World Trade Corporation is a Frenchman, the chairman of Standard Oil of New Jersey a Canadian.

Some American companies are electing non-Americans to their boards of directors (although in some categories of defense-related industries this is prohibited by U. S. law). Chrysler International is a Swiss corporation whose board, in accordance with Swiss law, has a majority of Swiss nationals.

Another visible trend is for American banks to team up with European banks in joint ventures or partnerships. Of three groups of banks bidding for the right to finance the construction of the English Channel Tunnel in late 1968, two included American banks. [13] The trend to transatlantic corporate partnerships is not confined to banks; two great hotel chains, one British (Trust Hotels) and one American (Western International Hotels), exchanged large blocks of stock in 1967 and planned various joint activities. However, when British Petroleum and Standard Oil Co., Ohio, tried to merge in the fall of 1969, the U. S. Justice Department blocked their way. U. S. antitrust challenges to foreign firms making American acquisitions have been relatively rare, but in this case BP and Sohio ran afoul of established policy which stipulates that companies which are substantial factors in any one market will not be allowed to merge. Ultimately, the merger took place, but not before British public and official opinion had been roused to sharp protest. International mergers are beginning to take place on the Continent, too, but also frequently with difficulty. A full merger of Fiat and Citroën was blocked by the French government in 1968. In most cases, so far, European companies have considered it more in their interest to merge with other firms of the same nationality, or with U. S. companies.

The most important point in assessing the "multinational-

[13] *The Times*, London, October 24, 1968.

ity" of any of these enterprises is the center or, to use a legal term, the locus of their ownership and control. The stock of most corporations is freely available on the various exchanges. Therefore the pattern of stock ownership in many large companies today tends to be international. European portfolio holdings in the United States, currently more than $10.5 billion, constitute substantial participation. But majority ownership and control still rest primarily with men of one nationality.

Many corporations, even those which have 100 per cent host country management abroad, prefer to retain 100 per cent, or at least an overwhelming percentage, of home control. Most prefer at least 51 per cent home ownership. Yet some major companies, such as ALCAN Ltd., operate a range of foreign subsidiaries in which the share of ownership varies from 10 to 100 per cent.

The more multinationalization takes place, the more it will do to damp down economic xenophobia. But this would not be the most important contribution multinational corporations could make: even in their present stages, companies with extensive overseas operations constitute a counter vailing power to the nation-state, a force which might eventually press hard for the effective structuring of interdependence.

Drucker sees the multinational corporation as the only institution "visible on the horizon that creates a genuine economic community transcending national lines, yet respectful of national sovereignties and local cultures.[14]

The creation of truly multinational corporations would also help to cure a prevalent form of corporate schizophrenia. For the attempt by national corporations to play an international role often results in a dilemma: they try to attach a kind of national coloration to their local subsidiaries, yet if this goes so far as to put key management decisions in local hands, it may hamper efficiency of a worldwide operation.

[14] Note 5, p. 97.

Until multinational ownership and management become much more common, much could be done to rationalize the movement towards economic interpenetration. It would help greatly if there were common regulations—or at least parallel national regulations—throughout the Atlantic system to govern the operation of international companies. Antimonopoly laws and guarantees against uncompensated expropriation would be standardized. Rules regarding foreign investment would be harmonized, especially regulations which cover the floating of stock and bond issues to raise capital abroad. Common patent laws to cover the entire Atlantic area would smooth the way for more economic integration. If these things were done the adoption of an Atlantic-wide or worldwide "multinational company law," as some have proposed,[15] might not be so important. In fact, if such an international law were adopted before there were a good many true multinational corporations (with about as many resulting from European as from American initiative), the overall results might be negative. Europeans might look upon the new statutes as simply another American Trojan Horse—a way to penetrate the Common Market still more easily.

There is another serious question: what government or authority would go to bat for a multinational company when its holdings, say, in Peru are expropriated? An alternative procedure might be to encourage the Common Market countries to adopt their own multinational company law (which they have been discussing anyway), to harmonize this with U. S. legislation, and eventually to achieve Atlantic-wide agreement on a common statute.[16] A start could be made by extending Common Market "rights of establish-

---

[15] See, for example, George C. Ball, "Cosmocorp: the Importance of Being Stateless," *Atlantic Community Quarterly*, Summer 1968, pp. 167–170.

[16] In an earlier era, the United States faced the same problem. As U. S. corporations became truly national, states began to compete for their location and the federal government was constrained to take on more general tasks of regulation. Nor is the U. S. economy yet fully integrated; there are, for example, considerable discrepancies in corporation taxation among the several states, distorting the operation of economic principles of efficiency. Witness to this is the fact that corporations choose with care the state in which they are incorporated.

ment," already in operation, to all the other Atlantic Countries.

There is a strong case for some kind of action. The United States and other governments today tend to think of the big international companies as "American" (even though by no means all of them are) and their activities abroad are often regarded as "invasion." The men in charge end up uneasily with allegiance to several sovereigns. Conflicts arise, inevitably, on such issues as East-West trade,[17] antitrust provisions, or on the reinvestment vs. the repatriation of profits.

THE CASE FOR COORDINATING THE ATLANTIC ECONOMY

The multiplication of nongovernmental economic ventures and linkages across borders at present is outrunning our capacity to deal with its consequences at governmental level. Governments are tending to respond separately and defensively in ways that endanger even the existing means of cooperation. To take two examples:

1.   U. S. legislation requires firms trading on American stock exchanges to disclose important details about their business. Many foreign companies are reluctant to do this, yet the Securities and Exchange Commission, under its interpretation of the law, attempts to extend its jurisdiction over them. Directors of foreign firms who do not comply, as the regulations now stand, can be prosecuted if they set foot in the United States. The other side of this question is that European firms sometimes find that the disclosures required by the SEC are actually helpful to them in their public relations at home.

2.   West Germany has a new law regulating mutual funds which is quite different from analogous U. S. legislation. If the two are not made compatible, the result could be conflicting, confusing regulations that pose an effective barrier to the flow of investments.

---

[17] The Belgian subsidiary of an American company recently got into difficulty with both the U. S. and Belgian governments over shipments of goods to a Communist country; U. S. subsidiaries in Canada have at times faced this dilemma.

Such anomalies, with respect to patents and licensing, competition, taxes (for individuals working abroad as well as for corporations), industrial and agricultural safety standards, social security and personnel practices, the transferability of currencies, and quite a number of other important aspects of doing business, are increasing and bringing nearer the day when the governments of the Atlantic powers must either say, "We give up—let it develop as it will and we will each individually simply stop whatever seems particularly offensive to us," or "Let us together put some system into the disorder, promote the underlying integrative trends, and see that the good of all is protected and the best ends of our peoples served."

Economic Policy Competition

Some may delude themselves by thinking that measures such as the Common Market or the Kennedy Round, because they constitute a sharp and encouraging reversal of prewar beggar-thy-neighbor international economic practices, have pretty well eliminated economic competition between governments. They have not. To be sure, contemporary competition between national economic policies is not so obvious as it was in the round of tariff increases in the late 1920's or the competitive depreciations of the early 1930's. But more subtle methods can be substituted, such as government procurement rules which favor home suppliers (including the various "Buy American" provisions) raising or lowering interest rates to obtain a brief advantage, credit-risk guarantees for exports, tax incentives, changes in the national tax structure or "voluntary" quota arrangements. Taken in sequence by different countries, these kinds of measures produce what economist Richard Cooper calls a "ratchet effect."[18] The result can be the same as if the countries had been devaluing their currencies competitively—

[18] *The Economics of Interdependence: Economic Policy in the Atlantic Community* (New York: McGraw-Hill, for the Council on Foreign Relations), New York, 1968, pp. 160–173.

clearly seen now as one historic road to economic disaster.

In graphic terms, Cooper portrays what can happen in such a situation:

One jurisdiction gropes around for new instruments in an attempt to improve its position. If it succeeds, others follow and there is a competition in policies which defeats everyone's objectives and in fact can even lead all participants *away* from their national or local objectives, like the members of a crowd rising to their tip-toes to see a parade better, but in the end merely standing uncomfortably on their tip-toes.

The rules of GATT[19] and other international bodies do not fully prevent the more sophisticated forms of "policy competition." As the world economy becomes more interdependent, these indirect pressures are likely to become greater, calling for better mechanisms of coordination. The common interest lies in increasing, rather than restricting, the mobility of productive resources.

The Choice

Are not these "better mechanisms" just a euphemism for giving away national freedom and sovereignty? It depends on your definitions. Continuing down the road we are now traveling, growing interdependent willy-nilly, we are gradually losing control over our economic future whether we like it or not.

The choice before the Atlantic countries is this: Do we let the increasing interpenetration of our economies grow *ad hoc*, so that we end up with a piecemeal, helter-skelter sort of integration in which the international business community steers its way as best it can? Or do we pull back in the direction of our national borders so that each nation can try to re-establish its freedom of action to decide separately what is good for it? Or do we follow a policy of undergirding international economic integration with a set of common

[19] The General Agreement on Tariffs and Trade, with headquarters in Geneva.

institutions adequate to guide and encourage the power and direction of international economic activity for our common public good?

If we pursue the first course, we simply put off the day of reckoning, for without government on a scale to match intercontinental activity, economies will inevitably clog up and the public interest will suffer. It is inconceivable that we adopt the second course, although now and then people talk as if one seriously could. The third course seems the only one logically open.

The OECD—An Instrument for Coordination

If, to avoid mutually destructive competition between national economic policies and to prevent nongovernmental economic integration from running away with itself, we adopt the course of insuring coordination by means of suitable institutions, then what policy instruments are at hand?

The obvious place to start is with the twenty-two member OECD (Organization for Economic Cooperation and Development), least glamorous of Atlantic institutions. Most of its creative work hides behind dry-as-dust rubrics such as "Policies for Part-Time Employment," "Tensions in the International Payments System," or "Improving Safety in Road Transport." But, for the Atlantic system as a whole, OECD represents the principal institutional backbone for shared governmental concern about economics.[20]

OECD's chief value—indeed its indispensability—to the Atlantic countries lies in its capacity to coordinate the various components that together make up the "economic policies" of its members. The shaping of national budgets, the introduction of tax changes, the treatment of unemployment, and many other matters we have been conditioned to think of as domestic are aired thoroughly in OECD and national difficulties bared for international inspection.

[20] In addition, the IMF, Bank for International Settlements, and Group of Ten play key roles in monetary affairs, along with OECD's Working Party III. In the next chapter we deal with this field.

Often, a country's plans and policies are changed as a result of what other members or the OECD secretariat has to say about them. A "Working Party" of the OECD, for instance, played an important role in the 1967–68 U. S. and U. K. balance of payments crises, bringing individual countries together on a common position and setting the tone for actions and reactions by debtors and creditors.

Many point to EEC and EFTA, both of which have eliminated restrictions on industrial trade among their members, as having accomplished more than OECD. But although OECD is neither a free trade area nor a customs union, in some ways it is more, for it deals with the stuff of national economic policy. As the classical barriers to trade—tariffs and quotas—become less important, the more subtle methods of protectionism gain in importance, and these are the meat of OECD.

A knowledgeable international economist has called "OECD one of the most hopeful, yet one of the most pitiful, creations of the postwar period."

OECD is hopeful for the reasons we have given: it represents a kind and degree of intergovernmental collaboration which are new in the international arena, and these forms of cooperation have worked surprisingly well.

But for all that it has accomplished, OECD is weak. It has a good deal of influence, but little power. It works well as a consultative body, but has only limited provision for decision-making. Consequently, as the OECD governments become increasingly involved economically with one another, and the need to make some joint decisions arises, they do not find OECD equipped for this role. Whatever effectiveness it enjoys is by persuasion rather than by vote. In this respect it suffers from the same limitations as NATO and other organizations to which nations have not yet been willing to surrender any real sovereignty.

OECD suffers also from a puzzling membership dilemma. Originally a western European organization, as the administrative agency for the Marshall Plan, it became "Atlantic" in 1961, when the U. S. and Canada became full members. In

1964 Japan joined, reflecting her emergence as great industrial and financial powers.[21] Australia participates in the work of OECD's Development Assistance Committee (DAC). Yugoslavia participates in some of OECD's working parties. Why should not both Australia and New Zealand, for example, be full members? They are Pacific countries, far from Europe, but so is Japan; and Australians and New Zealanders are more Western than the Japanese. Mexico, a North American country of 40 million people, has "taken off" economically; should she not belong? Should OECD consist of all the industrialized countries of the non-Communist or, at any rate, non-Soviet world? This is the way things are tending. Should OECD be geared to regionalism (more or less overlooking the Japanese case) or to a set of common economic problems? OECD is sure to face recurring *crises d'identité* of this sort as time goes on, with the economic, political, and geographic desiderata often conflicting. No easy rule of thumb suggests itself. The case of the OECD is a prime reflection of the complexity of the world's economy and the intricacy of its political relationships. But its very flexibility can allow it to adjust to the flow of a changing economic environment, if governments want it to.

OECD could use more vigorous leadership, by its member countries and its staff, to exploit to full advantage the framework that is already there. It might usefully get more fully into the trade business, dealing with some matters of principle prior to referring them to the operating forum of GATT, and attacking vigorously non-tariff barriers. Undoubtedly, OECD could be improved in many ways. It may not meet all the structural requirements of the kind of integration-oriented economic grouping which the 1970's call for, but it remains the most useful arm the Atlantic system now has with which to pave the way for the economic future and to resolve present difficulties.

In the meantime the private sector, through the growing

---

[21] Herman Kahn and Anthony J. Wiener in *The Year 2000* (New York: The Macmillan Co., 1967, p. 30) estimate that by the late 1970's Japan's gross national product will be larger than those of West Germany, France, or the United Kingdom.

multinationalization of business, presses ahead of governments to make maximum use of productive resources almost regardless of frontiers, to meet human needs and spur economic growth.

SUMMING UP

The national economies of the Atlantic area are more alike and better managed than ever before, but they are suffering from attempts to preserve national freedom of action in the face of new problems and prospects which clearly require stronger coordinating machinery.

Under the impact of advancing technology and the formation of large supranational markets in Europe, an interlocking Atlantic economy of great power and potential good is coming into being. A main instrument of integration is the international corporation, with command posts in several countries. However, such vast enterprises threaten to outrun the capacity of national governments to keep economic order and provide an encouraging climate.

In the 1970's it appears certain that the Atlantic powers will face an increasing need to overhaul, update, and augment their methods and institutions for economic coordination. The OECD, the instrument most readily available to meet this need, has done valuable work but it is not yet strong enough to serve the growing Atlantic business community or mediate the increasing competition in economic policy between national governments. Its future strength will depend in large part on the willingness of governments and private enterprise to give it greater powers and to use it more fully. Human wants and private initiative will seek new ways to move ahead when governments are too slow to act.

CHAPTER 5

A New Monetary Outlook

Thus gold, originally stationed in heaven with his consort silver, as Sun and Moon, having first doffed his sacred attributes and come to earth as an autocrat, may next descend to the sober status of a constitutional king with a cabinet of Banks; and it may never be necessary to proclaim a Republic.... The friends of gold will have to be extremely wise and moderate if they are to avoid a Revolution.[1]

J. MAYNARD KEYNES

A dozen years after World War I, a monetary crisis wrecked the laboriously rebuilt economic structure of the Atlantic countries. Recently, once again, the Western world has faced a monetary crisis threatening to upset the prosperity and equilibrium achieved by a quarter century of remarkable recovery from the even greater devastation of World War II. Speculation and inflation, high interest rates, and doubts about currency stability have been reminders of the boom of the 20's—which was the forerunner of the great depression of the 30's.

Once again there has been a gold crisis, and again we have heard paraphrased the cry of William Jennings Bryan seven-

[1] Quoted in the *New York Times*, Dec. 17, 1969.

ty-five years ago: "You shall not crucify mankind upon a cross of gold."

These events have put to the test the monetary mechanisms developed in these postwar years and have led to a series of striking innovations in monetary arrangements.

In this span of years the management of money has become much more a conscious art, if not a science. Vast changes have taken place in both the theory and practice of the control of money. In each of the Western countries the role of the central bank and of fiscal policy as instruments for economic stability and growth have been widely recognized, and methods have been devised for the use of those tools to serve human welfare. Even more important has been the recent development of international institutions for reaching mutual understandings and taking joint actions.

NATIONAL VERSUS INTERNATIONAL PROBLEMS

To understand these changes it is first necessary to distinguish between the more immediate national problems and the long-term underlying international developments. Recent situations in the United States, the United Kingdom, and France have clearly reflected emergencies which may be thought of as inherently national. For example, the economic crisis in France in 1968, under the impact of which that country lost $2 billion of its central bank reserves within a few weeks, was a domestic crisis resulting from student riots and a massive labor revolt. No monetary system is wholly proof against that kind of economic convulsion.

Equally, the monetary crisis of the United States was a direct result of huge Government spending at home and abroad, reflecting partly the war in Vietnam added to already large overseas commitments.

Similarly the political-financial situation of the United Kingdom reflected a failure of domestic policies to deal vigorously enough with inflationary trends, together with a longstanding balance of payments weakness from heavy overseas obligations.

While events of this sort have called for international intervention of one sort or another, they are not in themselves the long-term problem. Back of these immediate situations there are trends and problems which worsen and make more difficult the immediate crises.

GOLD AND MONEY

One way of describing today's basic monetary problems is to state them in terms of the relation between gold and money. For the monetary system today is based too much on gold, and problems arise from the fact that the world's supply of gold has been increasing in recent years much less rapidly than the world's requirements for money and credit. Thus the question is how to assure the growth of the money supply so that it is adequate, though not too large, and how to free ourselves from the dominance of gold.

The fact is that for a number of recent years the additions to monetary reserves from the production of gold were about 1½ per cent a year, and in 1967 and 1968, monetary gold reserves actually declined. But the world's trade has been increasing by leaps and bounds, something like 7 per cent a year.

The following diagram shows the known additions in the past fifteen years to the supply of gold, and the amount going each year into the monetary reserves of Western countries. As indicated, these countries in 1966, 1967, and 1968 were not able to make additions to their gold reserves. The entire amount of gold produced was absorbed commercially or for speculation or hoarding.

So the problem is how to meet the need for increasing bank reserves without relying on new supplies of gold.

How It Has Been Done At Home

Astonishing progress has been made in freeing domestic monetary systems from the bondage of gold. The United

States has by several steps passed legislation to reduce, and finally eliminate, the legal requirement of gold reserves in the Federal Reserve System. The System currently holds gold reserves equal to about 15 per cent of its total deposits and note circulation, compared with 60 per cent twenty-five years ago. To supplement its diminished gold, the System holds large amounts of U. S. Government securities.

While the techniques are different in other parts of the world, the industrial countries have found ways of releasing their money supply from any fixed relation to the amount of their gold reserves. This great change has been accepted because it has occurred gradually and people have learned that modern business is done by the use of bank deposits, credit, and checks, and not by coin or currency.

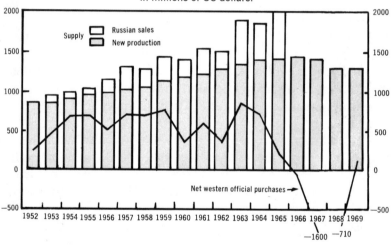

SUPPLY OF GOLD AND NET WESTERN OFFICIAL PURCHASES.
In millions of US dollars.

From Annual Reports of the Bank for International Settlements.

International Progress

It is the international problem of the relation of gold and money which has been more spectacular and more difficult to solve. But in this area also vast progress has been made.

As a prototype for these changes, there had developed, even before World War I, a mechanism for economizing on gold. The heart of the mechanism was in London, which was the center of the monetary and trading world. Businessmen everywhere were content to make London the world's bookkeeper, although the gold reserves in London were of modest size. Settlements for the world's business were done by bookkeeping operations in London. It was in effect a form of gold exchange standard, in which sterling exchange performed the function of gold in making settlements.

But after World War I, when the United States was coming forward as a banking center, making settlements was not so simple. Movements of money or gold had to be made between two or more centers, and London no longer enjoyed the same unique privileges and responsibilities as the world monetary center, and gold production increased less than the needs of trade.

New Problems and New Plans

Thus, after World War II, in fact even before the conclusion of peace, there began to be widespread recognition that new methods for effecting international settlements, and for assuring internationally valid money, had to be devised.

In the summer of 1944, financial leaders from the principal industrial countries met at Bretton Woods, New Hampshire, to work on these problems. The result was the creation of the International Monetary Fund, as well as the International Bank for Reconstruction and Development, both of which were adopted in 1945 by the principal industrial countries. (Russia and its satellites are not members.) The International Monetary Fund (the IMF) was an elaborate mechanism by which the member countries contributed to a pool of funds from which advances could be made to countries in temporary need to supplement their reserves. It was, in effect and within limits, a kind of Central Bank for central banks.

The plan of the IMF was so elaborate that at first many doubts were expressed about it. But gradually over the years, as it has accumulated experience and prestige, it has become an enormously valuable instrument, not only for supplementing the reserves of countries which were in need, but also as an agency for the analysis of economic problems of member countries and for providing sound counsel as well as money. It has been fortunate in the quality of its management which has constituted a corps for international leadership, something like the Commission of the Common Market. Its annual meetings have become the greatest assemblies of financial talent in the world, and its function as an informal organizer of opinion has become extraordinary.

The financial resources of the Fund, consisting of gold and currencies of its 120 member countries, have been increased by additions to each member's contribution, or quota, from an original $7.7 billion in 1947, to $9.2 billion in 1958, to $16 billion in 1965, to $21 billion in 1969. A still further increase of more than $7 billion was then pending.

With these resources the Fund has over the years made available from time to time the equivalent, in currency exchanges, of the sum of more than $20 billion—a large part of it now repaid. This action has on several occasions averted localized or general disaster. The Fund has also conducted hundreds of consultations, including the consideration and approval of many scores of adjustments in official rates of exchange.

There is one unique feature of the Fund's operations which has not been generally recognized. That is the extent to which it has certain supranational powers in such sensitive areas as exchange rates and advances to member countries. The twenty Executive Directors of the Fund have the power to take action in certain matters by votes weighted according to the size of each member's quota, without the necessity for securing unanimous agreement. In this respect the Fund is a trail blazer towards more effective international cooperation.

But this operation takes care of only one kind of need, and that is the temporary one. Advances of the Fund must normally be repaid in three to five years. Also, assistance by the Fund, except for limited amounts, is conditional on terms approved by the Fund. It does not supply the need for basic long-term reserves which may be obtained, held, and used unconditionally.

So the Fund's operations, valuable as they are, have not fully met the gap in basic reserves created by the limited amount of gold made available from new production, which in the past had provided a flow of funds into central bank reserves.

Distribution of United States' Gold

The impact of reduced supplies of new gold for monetary use has been eased by two special factors. The first of these is that for some time this gap has been partly filled by the gradual redistribution of more than half of the gold reserves which the United States had accumulated, so that its gold holdings over the past twenty years have been cut in half, from $24 billion to less than $12 billion. The gold reserves of European industrial countries have increased almost pari passu. This process has gone to a point where it has begun to hurt, and where the U. S. is reluctant to continue redistributing its reserves.

Growth of Gold Exchange Standard

Alongside the distribution of U. S. gold, another mechanism has developed for supplementing gold, and this is the wide extension of the "Gold Exchange Standard" in the form of U. S. dollars. Bankers and governments abroad have been prepared to consider as reserves dollars which they have earned or which they have borrowed. So the Central Banks of Europe now hold over $15 billion in U. S. government securities, bankers' acceptances, or deposits in U. S.

banks, which they consider, and report publicly, as a part of their reserves along with gold. Large additional amounts are held by private banks and businesses. Their confidence in these balances rests on the excellent long-term record of the United States in maintaining its currency at a fixed gold value, on its vast economic strength, and on the usefulness of dollars all over the world as a purchasing medium. Dollar balances also draw interest, latterly at high rates.

But this use of dollars as reserves, which goes under the name of the Gold Exchange Standard, has begun to be questioned. There is beginning to be reluctance on the part of Central Banks in Europe and elsewhere to keep accumulating more and more dollars, as the gold reserves of the U. S. have been shrinking, and as the U. S. balance of payments has been out of equilibrium.

Also there is legitimate question as to how sound it is for very much more of the world's reserves to be concentrated in any single currency. It is one of the curious anomalies of this situation that while Central Banks and governments hesitate to increase their dollar holdings, a new and large market for dollars has developed under the name of Eurodollars.

The changes in a ten-year period in the free world's monetary reserves are shown in the following table . The figures for reserve positions in the IMF represent the sum of the "gold tranches," that is, the amounts the member countries can withdraw without conditions, equal to what they had contributed in gold or convertible currencies.

World Reserves
(in billions of U. S. dollars as of mid year)

	1958	1968
Gold	38.	40.
Dollars	9.6	18.
Sterling	5.9	7.5
Reserve Positions in IMF	2.6	5.7
Miscellaneous	2.	2.
	58.1	73.2

Looking ahead to the next decade, no one of these sources of reserves seems likely to provide enough additional reserves to finance expanding trade, nor can further substantial shifting of gold reserves from the United States to other countries be expected.

NEW PLANS AND DEVICES

Under these circumstances much effort has gone into devising new methods for supplying reserves. One of these methods has been to strengthen the resources of the IMF, and this has been done, as noted above, in successive stages, through increased subscriptions by member countries. Similarly the operating principles of the Fund have been modified to make its aid more easily available. The principal industrial countries, the so-called Group of Ten[2] which now includes Japan as well as the Atlantic countries, have pledged themselves under certain conditions to make loans to the Fund (to an equivalent of $6 billion) through a plan called the "General Arrangements to Borrow," to take care of emergencies.

In addition, the principal Central Banks have agreed to make substantial temporary advances to each other for short periods, by exchanging one currency for another in so-called "swaps." This facility was put to use very heavily to take care of flights of funds from England and France.

Special Drawing Rights (SDR)

More importantly, negotiations within the Fund and among the principal industrial countries have resulted in agreement on a plan for "Special Drawing Rights." This

[2] Group of Ten countries includes Belgium, Canada, France, Federal Republic of Germany, Italy, Japan, the Netherlands, Sweden, the United Kingdom and the United States. Switzerland is a partial participant. The financial officials of these countries have been consulting regularly and frequently for many years at meetings of the Bank for International Settlements and the OECD.

plan was approved in principle at the meeting of the Governors of the Fund in Rio de Janeiro in September, 1967, and, final implementing action was taken in October, 1969.

These Special Drawing Rights are a new kind of asset. They take their value first from the fact that they are deliberately created by the Fund (and its members), as a responsible international body, in more or less the same way a bank puts deposits at the disposal of its customers. The new assets are allocated to member countries in proportion to their quotas in the Fund. These drawing rights do not have to be repaid like bank loans, though over a period a country agrees not to keep in use for making settlements more than 70 per cent of its allocation. The gold value of the S.D.R. is guaranteed and it bears interest. Further, the other participating members of the Fund have agreed to accept drawing rights from other members in making settlements.

The amount of SDR created was $3 ½ billion for the first year, 1970, to be followed by $3 billion in each of the two succeeding years. After that the amounts created are to be decided by vote of the members.

To sum up, the new Special Drawing Rights have the qualities that entitle them to be counted and used as reserves like gold or other reserve assets. They are a convincing supplement to gold reserves, and to that extent represent a further step towards gradually breaking the fetters of gold because they provide for an orderly growth in Central Bank reserves without reliance on additional supplies of gold. In the management of these special reserves, the Fund exercises certain powers which justify the expression supranational.

A Double Price for Gold

While these matters were under active discussion in the Spring of 1968, a panicky upset took place in the market for gold, with a huge speculative demand driving the price to $44 an ounce. While the immediate cause was the devaluation of sterling exchange, along with serious weakness in the U. S. balance of payments, these temporary factors brought into focus the longer-term problem of the adequacy of reserves. At a dramatic meeting in March, 1968, representatives of the seven Central Banks responsible for the London gold pool decided, acting on behalf of their governments, to separate the commercial market for gold from the gold transactions of the Central Banks.

Under this plan prices for gold in the open market would be free to react to supply and demand, having available new gold production. The Central Banks, on the other hand, taking into account the prospect of availability of the SDR, stated their belief that the $40 billion worth of gold now held by Central Banks constituted an adequate settlement fund for transactions among themselves. They announced that they had no need for buying more gold, and they undertook not to sell their gold in the open market. Transactions among Central Banks would continue to be at $35 an ounce. It was contemplated that required additions to Central Bank reserves would be provided by annual increments of Special Drawing Rights. The group requested other Central Banks to join them in this policy and obtained substantial agreement.

This action on gold, together with the Special Drawing Rights, may be said largely to have demonitized new gold production, but not the amounts now held by Central Banks. Also, the freeing of prices in the commercial gold market provides some inducement for increased production, as well as safeguarding the official price for gold. A satisfactory working arrangement has been achieved with the principal gold producers, under which the IMF will purchase limited amounts of new gold at not more than $35 an ounce. The market response to these moves, after some hesitation, was a gradual decline in the "free" gold price to around the $35 official price.

WHERE THIS ACTION IS LEADING

The net result of these drastic changes in monetary reserves will be to lead over the decade of the 70's to a quite different picture. It appears that ten or twelve years from now the amount of SDR in the world's bank reserves will be almost equal to the amount of gold so held. Gold will be a much smaller portion of total reserves and will be supplemented by the SDR.

In addition, foreign currencies, and particularly dollars will still be held as reserves. In the light of the experience with the Eurodollar, and added assurance from the new monetary program, central banks will probably be even more willing to hold dollars, and some other currencies, as reserves. So one could hazard a guess, looking forward, that the world's monetary reserves might consist of 1/3 gold, 1/3 SDR, and 1/3 foreign currencies and reserve positions in the IMF.

In this way the world's needs for basic banking reserves could be adequately taken care of for years to come.[3]

HOW ABOUT ADJUSTMENTS?

But this forecast of increased reserves does not supply a cure for economic adjustments between countries, which have been a major cause of recent difficulties. It is still true that countries which inflate their currency and overspend will find difficulty in getting and holding their share of banking reserves. And similarly, countries that are cautious in their fiscal and monetary policy and successful in their exports will accumulate more than their share of reserves. So the problem of adjustments has to be faced and is a constant concern of the Fund in its consultations and transactions with its members.

To meet this situation, proposals have often been made to

---

[3] We have been discussing here the world with free economics, as adequate information is not available for the Soviet or Chinese blocs.

correct maladjustments between currencies of different countries by allowing exchange rates to fluctuate more freely. The theory is that these fluctuations would tend to correct price level distortions and so bring into better balance exports and imports and capital flow. These proposals, while under continuing study, have not yet commended themselves to central bankers generally and others with operating responsibility. These bankers maintain that the flow of trade and investment depends on confidence in the value of the currencies with which trade is conducted, and fluctuating rates tend to undermine confidence and encourage speculation.

The statutes of the IMF provide for possible adjustments of currency values when they get out of equilibrium, but this facility has been used much less than originally contemplated, partly due to the reluctance of governments, for political reasons, to take the responsibility of either up-valuing or devaluing their currencies.

Many of the proposals for fluctuating exchange rates also fail to recognize the difference between the dollar and other currencies. The dollar, with its great strength and its link to gold, has been the fulcrum against which other currencies operate. Since most changes in currencies are downward (devaluation) caused by economic and political reasons, fluctuating rates, in practice, mean the worsening of the competitive position of the dollar.

The only way the dollar can compensate for declines in other currencies is to change its value against gold, and that means changing the price of gold. That would mean, in effect, changing the yardstick for the whole international complex of monetary arrangements. It would require Congressional action following long and unsettling debates. And it would probably not succeed in changing the relation between the dollar and other currencies, for they would be apt to move with the dollar. Any change in the price of gold ought to be made only for fully considered international reasons, and not to rescue the dollar.

As was demonstrated in France and Germany in the Spring of 1969, exchange rates have great political implications. Fixed rates are one of the best instruments for enforcing the economic discipline needed for economic growth and stability. Hence the reluctance of experienced bankers and officials to adopt the theory of fluctuating rates. But these ideas are nevertheless being carefully explored.

Another proposal worthy of further attention is that of Professor Robert Triffin of Yale University, for a system of "Gold Conversion Accounts" within the IMF, in which countries would deposit their dollar and sterling reserves beyond the amounts needed for intervention in the exchange markets. In Triffin's view, such accounts would supplement and strengthen the SDR and "pave the way to a gradual substitution of a truly international reserve system for gold as well as for the reserve currencies of today."[4]

New Instruments for Cooperation

Another, and more promising, means of improving the adjustment between countries is to carry further the procedures for bringing about mutual understanding and cooperation. The success of the IMF as an advisor and coordinator of international opinion suggests the value of still more moves in that direction.

Early in 1970, the Common Market countries announced formation of a "Common Monetary Reserves Pool." This action has a double objective: to provide resources for member countries running a temporary balance of payments deficit, and to tighten coordination among members on domestic goals, including a "tolerable rate of inflation."

This proposal invites the speculation that it might lead eventually to something like a European Central Bank and indeed a single European currency. What a blessing that

---

[4] Triffin's and other, more ambitious, proposals for monetary reform are presented in *Next Steps in International Monetary Reform, Hearing before the Subcommittee on International Exchange and Payments of the Joint Economic Committee of Congress* (Washington, D.C. : U. S. Government Printing Office), 1968.

would be for the traveller! Such a currency might in time rival the dollar as acceptable reserve money. Some kind of firm bridge with the dollar would surely be needed, so why not an "Atlantic" Central Bank?

The roadblock to this sort of ideal is, of course, national pride and political complications. Nothing is closer to the heart of sovereignty than the printing and control of one's own money. And fiscal and monetary policy are inseparable. Logical and desirable as it may appear, it will be some time before monetary policy becomes so fully international.

In the meantime one can be grateful for the vast strides taken in the past twenty-five years through the IMF and other agencies, including this recent European plan, to bring to monetary and fiscal decisions a clear consciousness of their wide international implications.

As one example, the extraordinary development of the Eurodollar market has been an unplanned revelation of the need for currencies which can flow freely over national boundaries. The extent to which the dollar has been so used is remarkable. This is evidence that steps already taken have begun to open up new freedom of movement in the money and capital markets.

So far, so good, but on the other side of the picture the currency emergencies of recent years have shown the sensitiveness of the world's money and the serious consequences which can flow from maladjustments between the economies of the great countries. For the foreseeable future we shall have to do the world's business with national currencies. World monetary policy rests still on the goodness of the money of individual countries. That in turn rests on the economic policies and strength of the major countries, and particularly on the United States.

Commenting on the forward strides achieved, a wit has observed that perhaps greatest progress has been made in international cooperation in money matters because politicians cannot understand the issues. The kernel of truth in this statement lies in the fact that nations have been learning to treat the management of money as a highly professional task and have entrusted it increasingly to Central Banks and related international institutions whose directors not only have special skill and knowledge, but also are a step removed from the give and take of political conflict. They have longer tenure of office than most office holders and have been learning how to work in harmony.

CHAPTER 6

Freeing Trade

To reconcile a scale of operations which is technically efficient with a scale of market which avoids the dangers of monopolistic domination, we need now to match the giant corporation with a free world market for its products. The national, and even the regional, free-trade market is no longer enough.[1]

J. E Meade

THE FREE TRADE CONTROVERSY

Since the late Middle Ages, Atlantic man has been arguing the pros and cons of free trade. We have gone through periods when barriers were complicated and excessive, and through other periods when they were minimal. In recent years, we have learned more in both theory and practice about the advantages of free trade and also more about the difficulties and disadvantages.

From an economic point of view, measured in terms of highest efficiency or greatest welfare for the greatest number, free trade is to be desired.

As trade barriers have continued to fall over the past

[1] Professor J. E. Meade of Cambridge University in a letter to *The Times,* London, July 11, 1968.

decade, trade has expanded phenomenally. The following table depicts this growth in terms of world imports in billions of dollars for the free-world countries for which figures are available.

WORLD IMPORTS
(in billions of U. S. dollars)

1961	124.6
1962	132.5
1963	143.5
1964	160.8
1965	175.1
1966	192.1
1967	201.8
1968	224.5

This increase is notable in that it has taken place despite a concurrent *decrease* in world reserves of gold and key currencies as a percentage of world imports. (This percentage dropped from 50 in 1961 to 34 in 1968.) The introduction of SDR in 1970 and after is designed to accelerate the growth of trade.

Much has been made of the advantages of free trade to lively, efficient export manufacturers, but little has been said about what it means to John Q. Public. Here is the recent view of Charles P. Taft, speaking to the Committee on Resolutions of the Republican National Convention, 1968:

Imports are the consumer's only real protection now against domestic inflation in many items. It has been true in automobiles: it works exactly the same in practically every important industry.

Resistance to free trade comes from producers who have difficulty in fighting foreign competition, or who would find it easier not to have to. In any country, there are inefficient producers who, unless they can become more efficient, will be forced out of business when trade barriers to outside producers are dropped. There are also industries which, because local or national conditions in one respect or another do not make for efficient manufacturing of a particular kind of product, are really uneconomic and actually cost the people of that country a great deal to sustain, in terms of excessive prices or other hidden subsidies.

In many such cases, the economist's answer would be for the country to get out of that particular line and put its resources into something for which its peculiar conditions give it a comparative advantage over producers in other countries. Yet, adjustments of this kind are difficult to make, in human terms. They can mean considerable unemployment, dispossession of entrepreneurs, and dislocation of whole communities or regions. It is natural, therefore, for industrial associations, labor unions, and groups of fearful citizens to resist the lowering of trade barriers if they believe the results will be harmful to them. The same pressures often combine to raise existing barriers.

The substantial elimination of trade barriers, as undertaken within the Common Market, calls for many adjustments on a scale which is changing the way of life of participating countries in important respects. There are not only the readjustments of individuals and groups, but all the nations involved are under pressure to harmonize many aspects of their economic life. Is there, for example, a clash between their taxation systems? Or their social welfare and security systems? Also, there are implications for defense; it would be more difficult for a nation participating in a free trade scheme to maintain its own separate system of defense production. So free trade, although almost certainly of great benefit to the large majority of people and national economies in the long run, also involves serious value judgments and difficult adjustments, including questions of defense, farm, and labor policy.

FREE TRADE AS A GOAL

Yet, for all the attendant problems, the goal of free trade still looks like a good bet for the Atlantic system and, on a longer time scale, for an even larger group of countries. There are caveats about timing and other measures which must be taken to make free trade produce the best results and to safeguard individuals and businesses, but experience with the two European free trade zones and the example of the flow of trade freely among the states of the U. S., have been moving industrial countries steadily in the direction of freer trade.

Events have pushed in this direction for twenty years. Freer trade seemed essential to inspire the recovery of western Europe after World War II. Tariffs have gone down everywhere in Europe, in the biggest and richest areas down to zero on industrial products. Import quotas there are minimal, and Europeans have not been hurt but on the contrary have thrived. The Common Market and EFTA show that the difficulties of adjustment to free trade have generally been exaggerated, at least in a period of expansion. In gauging progress, one must also recognize the stimulating influence of establishing such bold objectives as completely free trade.

When western Europe began to move towards free trade, the United States was itself pressed to take steps in that direction. The Kennedy Round negotiations (1964–67) resulted in removal of a large part of the tariff barriers to trade in industrial goods among all the Atlantic nations and many others. By comparision with the world of 1934, when the United States began to work for "trade liberalization" under the leadership of Secretary Cordell Hull, the freedom of trade today is phenomenal. In the words of two economists (who specifically except agricultural trade and a few other important commodities):

It is not an exaggeration to say that, insofar as tariff barriers are concerned, the limited goal of trade liberalization has now been achieved.[2]

---

[2] Theodore Geiger and Sperry Lea, "The Free Trade Area Concept as Applied to the United States," *Looking Ahead* (Washington, D. C.: The National Planning Association), October, 1967, p. 2.

Having done well, should we not do better and, as the Committee for a National Trade Policy has urged, move as far and as fast as possible towards general, completely free trade?[3] Despite the theoretical and practical advantages, this is not a question to answer lightly. So let us look at various aspects of it.

NON-TARIFF BARRIERS TO TRADE

Nation-states in search of economic advantage are cunning creatures. No sooner are agreements made with partners to drop customs duties than the treasuries and finance ministries, chambers of commerce, and other pressure groups are hard at work trying to work out schemes to nullify the effects of the cuts and put things back where they were. Or so it often seems. Such barriers to free trade are more indirect than high tariffs but can be every bit as restrictive, sometimes even more so. Some of the so-called "non-tariff barriers" (NTB's) that make the international negotiator's life miserable are:

> Health or standards legislation to which other countries are not geared.

> "Buy national" government purchasing regulations or policies.

> Tariff classifications which discriminate among foreign suppliers of a certain commodity. (A famous Swiss tariff regulation prohibited the import of dairy products made from milk of cows which grazed below a certain altitude.)

> Variations in customs valuation procedures.

> Dumping—selling abroad at lower prices than domestically—or discriminating anti-dumping rules.

> Regulations requiring articles to be marked with the country of origin, which sometimes adds greatly to cost.

[3] Committee for a National Trade Policy, Washington: Press Release of April 7, 1967.

> Aids to exports, such as low-cost export credit or government insurance.
>
> Excise and other taxes that discriminate in favor of domestic products.
>
> Restrictive trade practices, prohibited by other countries, which give one's own firms an advantage.
>
> Taxes in Europe on motor horsepower, and safety regulations in the U.S.

One other NTB, the import quota, limits the amount of a particular item which can be imported. Although widely used immediately after the Second World War, import quotas on non-agricultural goods traded among the industrial countries have been substantially reduced. One major exception is coal, importation of which the U. K. prohibits and some Common Market countries restrict. Another is oil imports into the United States. A good deal of Japan's trade with the West is restricted by import and export quotas, some by mutual agreement. Quotas remain more important in trade with developing countries; a number of Western countries, for instance, put severe quantitative restrictions on the importation of Indian and other textiles. Without the continuing firm discipline of a free trade area or customs union, there is always the danger that a business recession could lead to reimposition of quotas in a round of self-defeating attempts at protection.

Now that the Kennedy Round has reduced tariffs so that they no longer constitute a major obstacle to the free exchange of most industrial commodities, the proponents of freer trade have turned on the NTB's. Unlike bargaining on tariffs, negotiations on NTB's promise to be "difficult, prolonged, and unspectacular. They will have none of the simplicity and appeal of a clarion call to get rid of the tariffs by a certain date."[4] Many of the practices will be particularly difficult to eliminate, because while protective in their effect, they were originally adopted to serve some other, perfectly legitimate public purpose. Also, some NTB's will

[4] Isaiah Frank, "After the Kennedy Round," *Interplay*, April, 1968, p. 2.

open up fundamental questions of national economic or social policy. Finally, when some NTB's have by mutual consent been eliminated, we may confidently expect others—perhaps as yet untried—to take their places.[5]

Cutting back the vigorous undergrowth of NTB's is a task worth doing, however difficult. While the achievement of completely tariff-free trade for the Atlantic system will probably have to wait, for reasons we shall discuss later, movement on NTB's can begin now and will help the later progress towards free trade. Although the worldwide elimination of NTB's is desirable, the intricacy of the task suggests that the Atlantic nations plus Japan ought to work on it first, alone, and the OECD is the obvious forum.

FREE TRADE AND THE DEVELOPING COUNTRIES

Free trade arrangements among the industrial countries pose special problems in the others, often referred to as the less developed countries, the LDC's.

The United States for 45 years has followed the so-called "most-favored-nation" (MFN) principle in its foreign trade policy. MFN means, for example, that if the United States agrees with five other countries to drop tariffs from 20 per cent to 10 per cent on shoes, it will extend the same tariff cuts to any other countries.[6] This principle was incorporated into GATT rules in 1947. Under GATT (the General Agreement on Tariffs and Trade), the recent Kennedy Round, covering almost the entire scope of industrial products in the West, resulted in substantially lower tariffs for many countries—mostly less-developed—who had not taken part in the negotiations but who benefited nevertheless because of MFN.

However, even MFN—assuming that the industrialized

---

[5] Even with a high degree of economic integration, NTB's can still exist and prove troublesome to extirpate entirely. Witness numerous ingenious efforts, often successful, by states of the Union to restrict trade with their neighbors.

[6] But most-favored-nation treatment has not been extended by the United States to the USSR or to some other Communist countries.

countries were to go on with progressive "Round" negotiations—is not enough to satisfy the Asians, Africans, and
Latin Americans. They argue today: "You advanced countries are cutting down the trade barriers between you, and
you extend the same cuts to us. But this puts us at a disadvan-
tage because our manufacturing industries are young and
tender. What we need are *preferential* tariffs, letting our
goods into your markets with even lower duties than you
charge among yourselves. And don't expect us to lower our
duties, either."

If the non-industrial countries consider MFN inequitable,
then they would pose even greater objections to a free trade
area among, for example, all the OECD nations. By any
standard, such a free trade area would clearly discriminate
against the poor nations, because it would not necessarily
extend the tariff cuts undertaken among its members (eventually to zero) to any outside countries. This would make it
harder than ever for the manufactured goods of the developing nations to enter the West's markets.

For the southern hemisphere countries are using the old
"infant industries" argument, one traditionally employed in
northern lands and, so long as it does not result in permanent
protection for ineffiency, a valid consideration. To many in
the industrialized North, it might seem tempting to urge the
South to go on being hewers of wood and drawers of water,
providing raw materials for the North's industries, but those
days went with the exit of European colonialism. Today,
every new country wants its airline, its steel mill, and its
atomic power station, whether economically feasible or not.
These countries cite the evidence noted earlier, that many
industries can flourish almost anywhere, without much consideration for distance from raw materials or traditional
sources of power.

The Atlantic countries have recognized a mutal interest—
some would say an obligation—in helping the Asians, Africans, and Latin Americans industrialize. Although this may
mean added competition in industrial markets (and the

point has already been reached for some products, such as textiles or simple plastics), the economic growth of the West itself shows that industrial development breeds new consumers fast enough to absorb the added production. And, in terms of the West's self interest, the developing nations represent huge new markets for the future. Therefore, it clearly behooves the Atlantic powers, even aside from considerations of equity and justice, to help provide the poorer countries with some protection for their infant industries and at the same time offer their products progressively freer access to our markets, as we move towards free trade among ourselves. This one-way free trade would not always be one-way. Free trade area agreements should contain provisions for gradual elimination of the developing countries' remaining barriers, as their industries move out of the infant class; these might simply follow the West's scale of progressive reductions by a few years. In some cases, the developing countries' barriers to the West's products are excessive; many of these might initially be reduced in return for greater access to Western markets.

In a few Western industries, such one-way free entry for products from these countries might cause painful readjustment. The most obvious case is that of textiles; cheap goods from many LDC's already threaten to flood Western markets. Economist Bela Balassa, having studied the adjustments which would be required, asserts that to drop the West's bars to textile imports from developing countries would cause no great problem. He maintains that the amount of contraction necessary in Western textile industries could be accomplished without actually displacing workers, by gradually diverting new workers who would have gone into textiles into newer branches of manfacturing.[7] Within the United States itself, this is exactly what happened; New England textile mills could not compete with Southern plants closer to raw materials and employing lower-paid

---

[7] Bela Balassa, *Trade Liberalization Among Industrial Countries: Objectives and Alternatives* (New York: McGraw-Hill, 1967), pp. 170–171.

help. The result? Today New England manufactures electronic goods, advanced plastics, and other sophisticated products.

The advanced countries might couple the extension of temporary one-way free trade to the non-industrialized with encouragement of regional customs unions and free trade areas among groups of them. In the long run, such groupings (a few of which already exist, at least on paper) would stand to improve world trade because of the added economic strength they could give their members.

FREE TRADE AND THE COMMUNIST COUNTRIES

The effect of Atlantic free trade plans on relationships with the Communist countries is more difficult to calculate. Trade is looked on by the Soviet Union not solely as an economic question but also as a device for projecting its foreign policy into the outside world. More and more, however, Communist countries, including Russia itself, seem to be interested in trade for trade's sake. They have occasionally welcomed Western capital and managerial talent into their countries; Fiat will soon be making cars inside Russia.

The Atlantic countries must inevitably consider the question of trade with the East in setting up their own free trade system. For a free trade scheme that contained all but the Communist countries would probably, some day, be of interest to the Communist countries, and that prospect, on the right terms, should be kept open.

ALTERNATIVE STRATEGIES FOR FREEING TRADE

We have tried to make the economic case for free trade within as large an area as possible. However, the political considerations, which are probably overriding, and the alternative ways of eliminating trade barriers must also be scrutinized. No matter what form of free trade we would choose (and there are several), the question of timing is vital.

And this raises considerations which are largely political.

The United States has bet a great deal on the Common Market horse and the race is not yet over. Until now, any attempt to introduce free trade for all or part of the industrial world before the Common Market had gone much further towards uniting Europe economically would have seemed to run head on into the determination of the Six. To suggest at this stage that the United States join other countries in a free trade scheme without the Six—or even with them—might be interpreted as a hostile act by the Six and could tend to divide, not unite. the Atlantic system.

Current difficulties in achieving an EEC common agricultural policy, and in bringing about British entry, make the future of the Common Market and its relations with the rest of the Atlantic community difficult to predict.

But the Common Market still appears to be the most promising path towards greater economic cohesion in the Atlantic community. This does not mean that the United States or other countries outside the EEC need countenance unfair or unnecessary discrimination by the Common Market (now appearing with frequency), or that we must acquiesce in the EEC's attempts to set up its own broad preferential area which would be disruptive of wide attempts to free trade.[8] But it does mean that to adopt a trading policy which could be regarded as an attempt to break up the Common Market would not be a statesman-like act on the part of the United States.

With this important caveat in mind, let us now look at various alternative strategies for freeing trade.

Another GATT[9] Round.

The "Round" method, so far successful, has consisted in agreeing on percentages of reduction to be applied within broad categories of goods, over a period of years, and has

[8] Such preference schemes now cover a large part of Africa.
[9] GATT, the General Agreement on Tariffs and Trade, is formally a worldwide organization but in practice is more an institution whose motive power is Atlantic. The Kennedy Round was principally an attempt, using the GATT framework, to work out an Atlantic trading system.

been applied to nearly all industrial goods. The most recent one, the Kennedy Round, took three years and left some wounds. The agreed tariff reductions are now being digested in stages by the various parties. They will not take full effect until mid-1971. Theoretically, another Round could then be initiated, after we have had a chance to see the full effects of the 1967 concessions on all sides. The recent experience has, however, demonstrated the time, energy, and complications, both political and economic, involved in such an operation.

1. By the Round method, tariffs could theoretically be brought down to zero, but it would be more difficult under GATT than under a free trade area to be sure that they would remain there.
2. Negotiating parties resent the strains attendant on this particular type of bargaining.
3. The slower countries pace all the others.
4. The stubbornest obstacles, the non-tariff barriers, cannot be dealt with effectively in this kind of bargaining.

For these reasons, another Round would not be easy to get under way, nor necessarily successful even if started.

Sector Integration

This has been tried in the U. S.-Canada automobile free trade agreement and by the European Coal and Steel and Atomic Energy Communities. It consists in eliminating all tariffs and harmonizing other conditions of competition in certain industries over the course of a prescribed transition period. To extend this to Atlantic-wide or GATT-wide context would be a quite new idea. The difficulties are that: (a) there may not be many industries in which the principal countries have both protected and exporting sectors so that self-balancing agreements could be negotiated; and (b) the non-tariff barriers (for example, anti-trust legislation) might be very difficult to treat in isolation from the parties' other industries.[10] This type of action must still be considered in the experimental stage.

A Free Trade Area

There has recently arisen a movement with considerable political support, especially in England and Canada, for a North Atlantic Free Trade Area (NAFTA). This has been proposed as an alternative to British membership in the Common Market.

What is a free trade area?

The General Agreement on Tariffs and Trade (1947) provides for two exceptions to its rule that members may not engage in tariff-cutting and other trade liberalization measures that discriminate against other members; one exception is the *customs union* and the other is the *free trade area* . In the former, the participating countries, for trade purposes, form one country, with a common tariff barrier to the outside and no barriers to trade among themselves.

In a free trade area, the participating countries drop all tariff barriers among themselves, but each retains its own set of tariffs and other impediments to trade against outside parties. Until the first free trade area, the European Free Trade Association (EFTA), began in the 1960's to operate successfully, many students of the field had thought that, in the absence of a common external tariff, it would prove to be a practical impossibility. But EFTA has shown that free trade areas are feasible and can be effective.

A free trade area for the Atlantic system would bring its members many of the advantages enjoyed by members of the Common Market but with a wider scale of membership and hence more extensive benefits. The advantages claimed for this method include the following:

1. Because it would involve a lasting commitment to drop tariff barriers to zero and keep them there, it would encourage investors and firms to take full advantage of free trade.

[10] Sectoral integration is discussed by Frank, note 4.

2. It would require removal of restrictions in all sectors of trade, shifting resources to the most productive activities of each.
3. It would provide machinery for dealing with the NTB's.
4. It would provide mechanisms for eliminating controversies over customs valuing—a source of dissension which is diminishing the value of the Kennedy Round cuts.
5. It would stimulate world trade.

Possible disadvantages of an FTA would be the following:

1. Most less-developed countries, at this stage, could not join a free trade area. Unless the industrialized members of a free trade area were to accord one-way free trade for the products of the LDC's entering the industrial countries, the poor nations would be worse off than at present or under further "Round" cuts, as they now benefit at least from tariff cuts between the industrial countries, through the most-favored-nation provision.
2. To propose a free trade area now would interfere with efforts to integrate Europe, as noted earlier. Even if the Common Market countries were urged to join NAFTA at the outset, their answer today would probably be no. The British decision to try for a third time to enter the EEC shows clearly that the effort must take priority over any broader scheme. In terms of trade, the Six are more important today to the U. K. than the United States, EFTA, or even the Commonwealth. [11]

---

[11] U. K. exports to the EEC more than doubled between 1958 and 1964, whereas exports to the non-industrial Commonwealth hardly changed (Balassa, *note*, p. 18.). By 1966, British exports to the EEC were greater than to Australia, New Zealand, and Canada (the great bulk of Commonwealth trade) combined (Britannica Book of the Year, 1968, p. 760).

A PROPOSED COURSE

The Atlantic countries should adopt as a long range aim the creation of a free trade area among themselves, with arrangements for eventual membership by a still larger number of countries.

The economic and political arguments for such a movement seem compelling. The world is moving under the pressures of modern technology and imaginative thought towards a single economy, with the Atlantic system as its vital core. If this single economy comes about in an orderly way, men's living standards and opportunities could be greatly enhanced, far beyond present prospects. In the very long run, the political consequences of a free trade regime could also be positive: the chances are good that nations tied closely to one another by financial, commercial, and industrial interests will also develop stronger common political interests.

The United States, Canada, the EFTA and the EEC powers would have to provide the initiative, the motive power, and in the beginning the framework for this movement. The enlargement of the EEC to include the United Kingdom, Denmark, Ireland, and Norway would constitute an important next step. There would have to be an important place for Japan, and a way discerned at the outset for linking her position of leadership in the Pacific with the scheme. There should also be a system of temporary one-way free trade for as many developing countries as possible.

To set such a free trade arrangement as an ultimate goal would not require that the Atlantic governments act precipitously to realize the scheme; it could require decades. There are many reasons for proceeding deliberately; first, because not nearly enough is known about the possible consequences, economic and otherwise, or the various alternative paths to free trade; and second, because the economic and political situation in the Atlantic area is in flux and needs time to sort itself out.

But it is important to set an eventual goal of free trade as a guide to long-term policy and as a standard to repair to, as protectionist pressures (of late especially in the United States) arise.

CHAPTER 7

The Atlantic Community and the Asians, Africans, and Latin Americans

It becomes more apparent with every passing day that the interests of each nation and each man are inseparable from those of all others. It is now almost without reason to ask where one nation will be twenty-five years from now without at the same time asking where the world will be.[1]

LESTER B. PEARSON

HAVES AND HAVE-NOTS IN THE 1970's AND BEYOND

The rich nations, largely concentrated in the Atlantic system, are getting richer quickly. The poor nations, comprising most of those in Asia, Africa, and Latin America, are getting richer too, but at a slower pace. The gap between the two is growing, and it is unlikely that this trend will change in the 1970's.

As a group, the less-developed countries achieved an annual rate of growth in real gross national product of about 5 per cent in the 1960's, but much of this gain was wiped out by a high rate of population growth. In 1965 the per capita Gross National Product of the industrial world, in terms of available statistics, exceeded that of the less developed nations by a factor of twelve times. Herman Kahn and Anthony

[1] *UNESCO Courier*, February, 1970.

J. Wiener estimate that at the turn of the next century, this factor will approach a difference of eighteen times; and the gap will thus have increased heavily in favor of the developed world.[2]

If world population trends continue at the present rate, by the beginning of the next century there will be double the present number of people on the earth. Although revolutionary advances in agricultural methods—for instance in rice-growing—have been made, and it is possible that there will be unforeseen breakthroughs in fertility control, the next decade may still see great difficulty in feeding the people of the poorer nations. Until food production and economic growth decisively overtake population increase, we will not be out of the demographic woods.

The flow of assistance from the Atlantic countries in aid and investments is rising moderately in absolute terms, but decreasing as a percentage of the contributing countries' income.

From the point of view of either a humanitarian or a *Realpolitiker,* the outlook for closing the gap is anything but heartening.

THE BACKWASH OF COLONIALISM

The west Europeans were the first in modern times to reach out to other continents. With superior technology, more modern political systems, and restless dynamism they colonized most of the rest of the world in the four centuries up to 1900, brought dependent peoples some of the noble concepts and institutions of Western civilization and some of its less attractive features, and fought many of Europe's internecine wars among them. The European colonial system had largely come to an end by 1960, leaving a mixed heritage. Its demise, in part due to a growing thirst for freedom

[2] Herman Kahn and Anthony J. Wiener, *The Year 2000: A Framework for Speculation About the Next Thirty Three Years* (New York: The Macmillan Co.), 1967, pp. 142–145.

and self-determination, was hastened too because many colonies after World War II became economic and political liabilities rather than assets. Also, a moralistic United States, grown to power in two World Wars, pressed Europe to relinquish the "white man's burden."

Present relations between Asians, Africans, and "Europeans" (the usual African term for all whites, whether of Europe or not) have been impaired by the heritage of this colonial period, by the striving for new identity among emergent peoples, by their aspirations for the white man's technology and power, by their rejection of many of his values. Foreign assistance—the transfer of wealth, skills, and technical knowledge to these people by more economically advanced countries—is thus but one facet of a much broader, acutely complicated relationship with roots deep in history.

The need to relate the Atlantic system jointly to the southern half of the world stems first from long-range security considerations. If the main threat to the Atlantic system today comes from Russia, and tomorrow's threat could be China, then the day after tomorrow may see groupings of have-not countries threatening the world's fragile peace. Although the presently overwhelming technological and military superiority of the West may make such a prospect seem unlikely in even the medium-term future, developments in weaponry (much simpler and cheaper A-bombs, for example) or local strife could raise the likelihood considerably over a period of two or three decades.

In a recent book, Theodore Geiger states his belief that few Asian and African countries are likely to adopt Communism voluntarily or, if they become Communist, to submit to either Soviet or Chinese direction. "Indeed," says Geiger, "over the long term, the possibility is greater that—owing in part to the influence of Western messianism and redemptive activism—nativistic religious or political movements in Asia and Africa will generate the will and the ability to undertake sustained common action expressing racial antagonisms and cultural and economic resentments against the West."[3]

President Johnson's advisory committee on foreign aid, reporting in early 1969, put this case in perhaps more familiar terms:

> In American cities we have seen the costs of permitting the frustrations of poverty to drag on. Looking ahead to the long future, the committee does not believe that the United States can live securely in a world in which the poor countries are unable to raise living standards at least as rapidly as the rich countries—whatever the absolute gap in incomes.[4]

There are other excellent reasons for "doing something" about the LDC's (less-developed countries): our humanitarian ethic, the strengthening of the world economy, the protection of Western commercial and industrial interests which are of mutual value, elementary justice, and others— but Geiger's dark vision offers as good a justification as any. The idea of the world ending up in one vast racial conflict, blacks and yellows against whites, and have-nots against haves, is terrifying. To prevent such an ultimate catastrophe will take more than money or willpower or good intentions; it will require all the knowledge and enterprise the West can muster.

THE LIMITS TO AID

"Foreign aid" programs of the Atlantic powers have generally emphasized economic assistance, reasoning that if living standards can improve and productive capacities increase, these will lead to the rise of a middle class, the growth of democracy, the satisfaction of material aspirations, lessened discontent, and, ultimately, stable societies. But the snail's pace of change in these fundamentals in most countries

---

[3] *The Conflicted Relationship: The West and the Transformation of Asia, Africa, and Latin America* (New York: McGraw-Hill, for the Council on Foreign Relations), 1967, p. 259.
[4] Report of Presidential Task Force on International Development, March 8, 1969.

aided has given rise to Western disillusionment. Perhaps, some observers now say, "economic aid" is not the main answer.

Geiger reasons, "The obstacles are not simply, or even mainly, the scarcity of economic resources and technical skills. They are the characteristics of the transitional society itself, and the most important of them are not susceptible to rapid removal through deliberate policy measures." Probably the heart of the matter lies in the *motivation* of a society, without which there is neither incentive for internal capital formation nor attractiveness to outside investors.

Gunnar Myrdal concluded recently after an exhaustive study of economic development in Asia[5] that capital, savings, education systems, and technical know-how are all less important factors in development than the deepseated resistance to structural changes in the traditional societies of the East. To develop modern economies, these countries must adapt their habits to growth and change. Myrdal stresses the need for such modern attitudes as self-reliance, risk-taking, initiative, discipline, and self-help.

It is obvious that even if Western aid programs become far more sophisticated and generous, and even if the products of the LDC's enjoy freer access to Western markets, the prosperity and stability of the underdeveloped world could not be guaranteed by the West. Even if we were willing to quadruple our capital and aid flows, most of the problems would still prove intractable.

Making real progress in development may depend less on the sheer size of funds (although the present level of aid should be raised), but more in understanding by both suppliers of funds, and even by recipients of funds, of the histories and cultural and social characteristics of the LDC's.

Kahn and Wiener believe that if the non-industrial countries could learn how to use aid well and if the industrial countries would persist in putting regularly a more significant amount of their Gross National Product into aid (they

[5] *Asian Drama* (London: Penguin), 1969.

suggest one to three per cent), the accumulated momentum would result in "impressive sums . . . enough to get things started by the late 1970's and to make clear that development can occur."[6]

Of course, these are extremely large "if's."

PRESENT SCOPE OF ATLANTIC ASSISTANCE

To stress the overriding social and cultural complexities of development, to warn against expecting too much of foreign aid, and to suggest a fresh review of priorities is by no means to suggest that Western economic and technical assistance up to now has been ineffective. A considerable transfer of skills and wealth from the northern hemisphere to the southern by governments, businesses, international organizations, and private foundations has taken place and the results in some cases have been spectacular. Mexico, Taiwan, and South Korea are among those countries which no longer require foreign aid, proof that the burden need not be endless. In an earlier era Japan "took off," and largely by its own efforts.

In quantitative terms, the Atlantic countries' flow of funds to the less-developed in recent years has risen more or less steadily, if moderately. The Development Assistance Committee (DAC)[7] of the OECD publishes the relevant statistics each year and they are shown in the Diagram on page 127 and in the table on page 128.

Figures for 1968 show a total flow (private as well as public), including loans, grants, and multilateral as well as bilateral aid, of $12.8 billion. This is an increase of about $1.5 billion over 1967, due entirely to increases from private sources.

---

[6] Note 2, pp. 253–255.
[7] Comprising Australia, Austria, Belgium, Canada, Denmark, France, Germany, Italy, Japan, the Netherlands, Norway, Portugal, Sweden, Switzerland, the United Kingdom, and the United States. The Commission of the European Communities is also a member. DAC carries out a thorough annual review of each member's aid policies, sets quantitative and qualitative standards for aid, encourages better coordination among donors, and tries to increase the impact of development assistance.

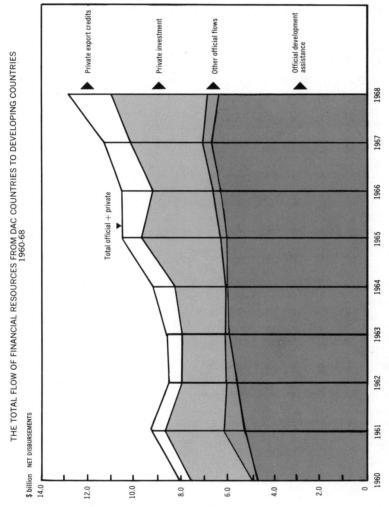

THE TOTAL FLOW OF FINANCIAL RESOURCES FROM DAC COUNTRIES TO DEVELOPING COUNTRIES
1960-68

$ billion   NET DISBURSEMENTS

14.0

12.0

10.0

8.0

6.0

4.0

2.0

0

1960   1961   1962   1963   1964   1965   1966   1967   1968

Private export credits

Private investment

Other official flows

Official development assistance

Total official + private

From the Annual Report of the Development Assistance Committee of the O.E.C.D.

U. S. funds comprised 45 per cent of the 1968 total, but in terms of ability-to-pay, measured by funds as a percentage of gross national product (GNP), the United States lagged behind the majority of DAC members: six out of sixteen met the target of one per cent of gross national product, but U. S. funds equalled only 0.65 per cent of its GNP. U. S. official aid has been declining, and under prevailing legislation will decline further. The private flow of funds is increasing in spite of adverse policies in some countries.

THE TOTAL NET FLOW OF FINANCIAL RESOURCES FROM DAC MEMBERS TO LESS-DEVELOPED COUNTRIES, 1960–1968
(including contributions to multilateral agencies)
Net Disbursements in Millions of U. S. Dollars

	1960	*1968*	1968 *% of* GNP
Australia	59	187	0.67
Austria	6	74	0.66
Belgium	182	243	1.15
Canada	145	306	0.49
Denmark	38	74	0.55
France	1,325	1,483	1.24
Germany	625	1,635	1.24
Italy	298	505	0.70
Japan	246	1,049	0.74
Netherlands	239	276	1.10
Norway	10	58	0.65
Portugal	37	74	1.45
Sweden	47	127	0.49
Switzerland	157	242	1.43
United Kingdom	881	845	0.83
United States	3,818	5,676	0.65
DAC Member Countries Combined	8,112	12,855	0.77

Countries which have exceeded one per cent of their GNP in the flow of assistance include Portugal, Switzerland, France, Germany, Belgium, and the Netherlands.[8]

To put these statistics in more intimate terms, the assistance flow from DAC countries has represented 22 cents per week per head of their populations.[9]

These figures include assistance flowing through several multilateral institutions including the United Nations Development Program (presided over by Paul Hoffman, former Administrator of the Marshall Plan), the World Bank (of which Robert McNamara is President), and regional banks for Latin America, Asia, and Africa. These institutions handle only about 10 per cent of the total flow of assistance from the Atlantic countries, but their value is much greater than that figure suggests. As multilateral agencies, in which the receiving countries have a voice in the operation, their influence for sound and successful practices is important and is freer from suspicion of political pressure than in the case of bilateral aid.

The above figures are exclusive of the operations of the International Monetary Fund which makes available resources to the less developed countries at times when they need it most. Several of the foregoing agencies are worldwide in their operations, but the Atlantic countries are by far the largest suppliers of funds, and technical assistance as well.

The flow from DAC countries to the LDC's amounts to well over nine-tenths of all financial and technical assistance received by the latter. Aid from the Communist countries, although it looms large in the press, and in a few cases has had important economic or political impact, is inconsequential by comparison.

[8] It is interesting that an important part of the French aid effort consists in furnishing about 40,000 school teachers and technical experts to LDC's, largely in former French colonies.

[9] Figures in this section came from an OECD Press Releases of July 11, 1969, and February 12, 1970, and from the *Survey of International Development*, Washington, D.C., July 15, 1968.

The report of the World Bank's Commission on International Development, headed by Lester B. Pearson, confirmed the overall figure of one per cent of GNP as a desirable target, to be attained "in no case later than 1975." The Commission recommended that each donor country strive to attain a level of official, as distinct from private, assistance of 0.70 per cent of GNP. To reach the Commission's aid target would require a sharp turn-around for many nations, including the United States, whose official development aid in 1968 totaled $3.3 billion, or 0.38 per cent of GNP. By 1975, the Commission estimated, U. S. official aid should be $8.2 billion, a massive expansion over President Nixon's request for 1970 of $2.2 billion.

Some countries are clearly growing weary of well-doing. Our review of the trends, both of prospects in the LDC's themselves and of the outlook for more aid from the West, does not encourage complacency. Even one per cent of GNP will be extremely difficult to attain. In the long run, aid will have to be largely replaced by trade and private investment. There are gains in both of these but gains are slow in relation to the need.

MORE EFFECTIVE AID

Foreign aid is not in the same category as those economic, defense, and political interests which the Atlantic countries generally regard as directly vital to their security. The case for foreign aid rests more on grounds of humanitarian and long-range self-interest, and therefore has little political glamor, though among insurgent youth aid to poorer countries has considerable support.

It is wise to recognize that there are limits to what the industrial countries can do about the "North-South problem" as we have described it. To close, or even narrow, the economic gap between North and South now seems impossible without either an unimaginable collapse of the Atlantic economy or a truly startling improvement in the LDC's; the latter is to be devoutly desired but hardly expected.

Nevertheless, the Atlantic countries have every reason to persist in their endeavors to increase and improve aid both because of good results achieved in economic, human, and political terms, and the long-term necessity for achieving peace and stability in the "third world" countries.

The OECD, through DAC, is proving to be about the best locus for stepped-up pressure on all Atlantic countries—and particularly those which now lag behind—to do more. The steady facing up to the needs and the results, and the comparison between what the different countries are doing is a stimulating influence.

Bilateral or Multilateral Assistance

A problem which all Atlantic countries face is that of multilateral vs. bilateral aid. The multilateral channels through such organs as the World Bank complex, the UN's Special Fund for Economic Development, and regional development banks, have the special advantage that the borrowing country often finds it easier to accept advice or stipulation of loan conditions from a multilateral agency than from a single country. Also the amounts that can be made available are often larger, and there are fewer limitations on where goods are purchased. While at present bilateral assistance is far larger than multilateral, the Pearson and other reports have all been favoring increased use of multilateral agencies. Both the World Bank and the OECD have development centers for the thorough and objective analysis of the economic and social problems involved.

Looking forward to the time when multilateral arrangements are likely to be more and more necessary to solve world problems, it is most desirable to accumulate experience through joint agencies for assistance.

TRADE VS. AID

In Chapter 6 of this book the advantage of according special trade arrangements to the developing countries was reviewed. It was suggested that the developed nations could well drop some of their barriers—such as quotas and high tariffs to commodity imports from the LDC's. Trade liberalization under the GATT has applied so far almost entirely to manufactures.

Perhaps the most effective way for the developed countries to reduce their obligations for rendering aid to the LDC's is to encourage a flow of exports from them. Fortunately this is already happening as shown by the following table. In the seven years since 1960, the rate of growth of exports from developing countries has nearly doubled for primary commodities and more than doubled for manufactured goods.

ANNUAL AVERAGE GROWTH RATE OF EXPORTS BY
DEVELOPING COUNTRIES* 1955–1960/1960–1967†

In Percentages

Annual Average	Primary Commodities	Manufactured Goods	Total
1955–1960	2.5	4.9	2.8
1960–1967	4.4	11.1	5.5

*Outside of Europe

TIED VS. UNTIED AID

A particularly nettlesome problem has grown out of the practice of some governments in giving loans or grants in the form of "tied aid," which requires that recipients use the currencies provided for purchases in the donor country. This is not always in the recipient's interest, as he might be able to buy exactly what he needs, or buy it more cheaply, in another country. It was estimated, for example, that tied aid

†Source: Handbook of International Trade and Development Statistics, 1969, UNCTAD, Geneva.

reduced the value of all outside capital received by Pakistan in 1965 by 12 per cent.[10] While such figures are not readily available, this case is plausible and may well be typical. Tied aid is indefensible in the case of countries whose international payments balances have been consistently in surplus. Critics have urged with justification that such donors make their aid convertible and expendable in deficit countries. In return for such liberalization, countries such as the U. S. and the U. K. would find it easier to relax their own "tying" practices. In both these cases, the tying of aid was adopted under pressure of serious balance of payments difficulties. The pros and cons of tied aid have often been discussed in DAC. The seriousness of the problem suggests that it deserves more determined efforts to find a solution.

THE PRIVATE CONTRIBUTION

The chronic dilemma of the developing countries is that their development cannot be done for them. They must achieve it themselves.

Certainly they will need much capital and know-how from outside, but the essential elements of progress—will and ability—must be developed from within. In this process, the developing countries face a formidable, puzzling complex of problems.

Myrdal put his finger on a basic difficulty, the deep resistance of traditional societies to change. Flowing from this fundamental disability are other problems, such as population growth, illiteracy, resistance to agricultural and industrial technology, and inhibitions against a modern market economy. Each of these problems interacts with the others. The pity is that so often popular leaders by unwise political action stifle the enterprise, both domestic and foreign, which is most needed.

Essentially, observes Drucker, the problem is not to parcel

[10] John Pincus, *Trade, Aid, and Development: The Rich and the Poor Nations* (New York: McGraw Hill) 1967, p. 310.

out scarce resources equally but "to make the poor productive."[11]

There is no panacea, but rather a tough complex of problems to be solved by a multiplicity of thoughtful approaches. Essential as the flow of private funds from industrialized countries is, it needs to be complemented by other approaches. Only public aid can build roads, communications, schools, and other public works which can never turn a profit but which provide the basic infrastructure for development. Government aid is also necessary to support certain important enterprises whose profitability lies somewhere in the future. But business enterprises, private foundations, and non-governmental bodies together have a major part to play.

The role of private firms and banks is increasingly important. Of the total net flow in 1968 from Development Assistance Committee members to LDC's of $12.8 billion, private enterprise contributed $5.9 billion or 46 per cent, though part of this represented credits with a government guarantee. Of the 260,000 expatriate experts working in LDC's in 1965, more than 60 per cent were from private enterprise. Of total exports of $40 billion from LDC's in 1967, three-fourths went to private concerns in industrialized countries.[12]

The Rockefeller and Kellogg Foundations are among several whose contributions to public health, agricultural development, and education in the Southern Hemisphere has been notable. The Ford Foundation has spent huge sums, by private standards, for a wide variety of pilot projects, studies, and educational efforts aimed at economic and societal growth. One of Ford's recent achievements was the successful introduction of a much-improved strain of rice which has dramatically changed the food outlook in Southeast Asia.

[11] *Note 5,* Chapter 4.
[12] Dirk U. Stikker, paper presented to the International Industrial Conference, San Francisco, September 15–19, 1969, as the result of an extended study for the United Nations of the private role in development.

The aggregate export-import gap of the LDC's is still widening adversely and their debt-service burden is increasing. One reason is because of wide fluctuations in the world market prices for their raw materials. Another is tariff barriers by developed countries against goods from the LDC's. A third reason is the propensity of many developing countries to try to develop "prestige" industries (such as steel mills) which cannot operate profitably in small markets or provide the exports essential to repay foreign capital.

Private enterprise may be contributing to LDC's far more technical assistance than governments. This is the cheapest and probably the most effective form of aid. With private investment goes not only capital but usually education and technological and managerial know-how for the creation of new industries.

Despite these manifold benefits which private investment has brought, and can bring, to the development process, many governments in LDC's continue to regard it suspiciously as "economic colonialism" or "exploitation." Discriminatory obstacles are put in its way. Expropriations frighten potential investors. Business consistently and understandably pleads for a better "investment climate" in the developing areas. Despite impediments, progress has been made in getting foreign investment to serve more directly the host countries' interests, and also in getting host country governments to improve the climate for investment, both domestic and foreign.

More can be done. In recent years, consortia of banks and industrial firms in several developed countries have been set up to furnish multinational investment to "capital-thirsty" countries, such as India, Greece and Turkey. The ADELA consortium, which grew out of an initiative of the North Atlantic Assembly, now operates in Latin America and is a case in point.

Another promising technique is that pioneered by the International Finance Corporation—a World Bank subsidiary—which puts funds provided by the Bank on an equity basis into private enterprises in LDC's in partnership with local investors and entrepreneurs.

SUMMING UP

The world is still divided between rich and poor, haves and have-nots. Broadly speaking, the poor are the countries of Asia, Africa, and Latin America. And the gap between this poor "South" and the rich "North" is growing larger.

In earlier times, this sort of discrepancy was considered "normal." Today all that is changed. There has been an explosion of expectations which the governments of the poor countries often are unable to contain. When such pressures explode into violence, the world's peace is threatened.

The Atlantic countries have a special responsibility in this situation. For it was they who reached out to establish colonies and exploit their natural resources, who brought to the "third world" new ideas of human dignity and freedom and smatterings of new cultures. No objective student denies that the process brought with it two-way benefits, but no matter what the balance of advantage today, the North awakened the South to general discontent with its lot. And independence from the North has not, as many assumed it would, brought in the millenium.

The Atlantic "have" countries possess wealth, knowledge, and a unique culture which attract others. Today they recognize their responsibility for the state of the "have-nots," partly because they want a stable, peaceful world, but also for economic reasons. Trade is to the mutual advantage of both the North and South. Also, the rich countries acknowledge today a humanitarian duty.

These motivations have produced a precedent-shattering program of assistance by the Atlantic countries and Japan to the poorer lands, amounting to a flow of $12.5 billion per year. The North has aided the South not only with money, but with human skills and education. A series of multinational institutions to coordinate and guide these flows has been set up. Massive private capital is also flowing to countries where it is welcome.

With such help, progress is being made: the gross national product of the LDCs is increasing at an average rate of about five percent a year. But this is in large part offset by a too rapid increase in population.

In this situation, most serious observers think the rich countries should do more. A flow of about one percent of GNP to the poor countries from the rich is now a widely accepted ideal. But those who study the problem also agree that the result depends much more on what the poor countries do for themselves in terms of enterprise, education, capital formation, birth control, capable public administration, social transformation, and the provision of an attractive climate for private investment, both domestic and foreign.

Better forms of mutual trade agreements, exchanges of scholars and students, joint scientific research, and other forms of international cooperation are also much needed.

While bilateral forms of aid will undoubtedly be a feature of the international landscape for some time to come, the value of multinational institutions as a vehicle for development is being recognized increasingly. The United Nations and its specialized agencies, the World Bank, the IMF, and the regional development banks have all proven their worth. For the Atlantic community in particular, the OECD acts as a most useful clearinghouse for ideas and methods and provides an international measuring-rod and a stimulus to further efforts. It could do still more if its member-countries wished.

But the world is facing a great wave of human emotions —of people who live in dire poverty and indignity, and who now know there could be something better. The seeds of bitterness and violence have been sown. No one can predict the harvest. The very best we can do is not good enough to be confident of the result.

PART III
Atlantic Political Future

The beginning of a modern Atlantic community arose in the mid-forties largely in response to a grave threat, the danger that Soviet Russia might absorb war-devastated Western Europe. In the fifties, with European societies and economies reasonably restored behind an improvised NATO shield, it was gradually perceived that the threat to Western security was global. In the 1960's, the danger came to be seen as going beyond the monolith of Soviet-dominated Communism, and was recognized as including the vast storm-tossed areas of an underachieving Southern Hemisphere.

Into the 70's and beyond, the Atlantic powers will be brought face to face in the South with such problems as the demographic explosion, the revolution of rising expectations, and the instability of weak governments. These problems will be exacerbated by the increasing capability and demonstrated willingness of the Soviet to fish worldwide in troubled waters. The extent to which China will figure seriously in this equation is largely unpredictable, but it is a formidable factor.

Thus for the present and the foreseeable future the shadow of the iron curtain falls over all the affairs of the countries of the Atlantic and other countries which subscribe to like principles and practices of human freedom and enterprise.

Still central to a precarious world stability is the balance of power in Europe between East and West. This requires the maintenance of clearly effective protective and deterrent forces, which will discourage any temptation to aggression. The appalling cost in resources and energy is a serious drain and diversion of attention and effort from many demanding economic and social needs.

For these and humane reasons the desire for peace, and for achieving a genuine peaceful co-existence with the communist countries is an over-riding sentiment in all the Western countries. They have made, and will continue to make, proposals towards this objective. But the response thus far has been meager and disappointing.

The concluding chapters of this book will review these political questions: the outlook for East-West accommodation; the present and prospective requirement for maintaining the necessary military strength; and the kind of political organization which will be most effective in the search for peace and international cooperation.

CHAPTER 8

The Outlook for East-West Accommodation

We witnessed first the Communization of the Balkans; we are now witnessing the Balkanization of Communism.[1]

LEO LABEDZ

INSIDE THE SOVIET BLOC

One often tends to think of the eastern European countries as homogenized by Communism; this is a superficial view. Most have in common their Slavic roots, but the similarities in language are no greater than that of Italian to French. If anything, the ethnic particularisms of Balkan Europe today are stronger, despite two decades of supposedly international Communism, than is centrifugal nationalism in western Europe.

Even within each eastern country unity can be a tenuous thing; Tito sits on a powder keg of subnationalisms; the Czechs and Slovaks still jockey for advantage. Some parts of eastern Europe, such as Albania or Bulgarian Macedonia, are extremely backward economically and politically; other parts, such as Czechoslovakia, are highly developed countries, comparable to the advanced nations of the Atlantic

[1] Cited in *The Atlantic Community and Eastern Europe: Perspectives and Policy* (Paris: The Atlantic Institute), 1967, p. 13.

141

system. Roman Catholicism and its traditions are especially strong in Poland.

Today, whatever unity exists among the east European countries is due in some part to Marx and Lenin, but above all to the iron-fisted rule of their Soviet overlords. Yet the unwillingness—or even inability—to stick to Moscow's pattern is becoming more, not less, apparent all the time. The desire to show independence from Russia, to bridge the gap between fair words and deeds, to achieve both justice and democracy, to find the coherence which will enable the socialist system to achieve its goals are all observable throughout eastern Europe.

But goals have not been reached. Living standards have not risen dramatically; production, especially in agriculture, has fallen short of targets; political, social, and human rights have not been guaranteed; relations within the Party are not free of conflict and the crass motivations which Communists have attributed to capitalists; the "national question," involving ethnic minorities, has not disappeared. Realization of these facts—widespread now in eastern Europe—has produced doubts, concern, unrest, and largely hit-or-miss attempts to cope with change.

Economically, changes in the Communist system have been considerable, especially in Yugoslavia. The defects of highly-centralized, rigidly planned, production-centered economies have become evident as the Eastern countries move into fuller industrialization and consumers begin to clamor for—and are not able to afford—a wide variety and stable supply of goods. Observers however do not interpret this development, suggesting the introduction of Western free-market principles, as indicating a swing towards Western political concepts; it represents rather the consequences of advancing industrialization. The Communist countries are simply coming up against problems already confronted, and at least partly solved, by the industrial West.

If Communism economically is no longer recognizable as the Stalinist model, neither is Capitalism the kind that Marx

wrote about. In many ways one can say that the two economic systems, East and West, are drawing somewhat closer
together. Great differences remain and the gap with the
West remains large in terms of production, popular consumption, and motivation.

It would be a mistake to think, however, that Western-
style democracy is on its way in these countries. Growing
numbers of intellectuals appear to want Atlantic liberties—
especially the right to speak and write one's mind—but the
idea of a one-party socialist state, based firmly on Marxist-
Leninist principles, holds sway.

Evident in some countries (particularly Czechoslovakia)
has been a desire to increase civil rights and to make the
political and economic system more flexible and responsive
to people's needs, but the idea of permitting a free interplay
of political forces, of allowing multi-party representative
government to flower, is still remote everywhere. The flash-
point for Soviet intervention—or for tightening the screws
in the USSR itself—is the appearance of anything which
might threaten one-party Communist rule.

The only eastern European country with a genuine tradition of modern democracy, Atlantic-style, is Czechoslovakia.
It is not surprising that post World War II liberalism has
asserted itself more strongly there than elsewhere in eastern
Europe. The great Atlantic revolutions of the eighteenth and
nineteenth centuries affected the other east European countries little, touched some not at all, and in almost all cases
met limited, if any, success.

From the point of view of artistic and architectural styles,
literary ties, religion (partially), and ancient and medieval
historical traditions, the eastern European countries defi-
nitely share the cultural spirit of the European continent
with the western Europeans. The western part of Russia—
more or less as de Gaulle has suggested, "to the Urals"—also
shares, but to a lesser extent, these attributes of Westernism.
(Russia was the principal heir to Byzantium, which split off
gradually from the main corpus of the West, beginning with

the downfall of Rome. There is much of Asia in Russia.)

In terms of the character and quality of its political culture, most of western Europe is today poles apart from eastern Europe. For the most decisive historical trend of the last four centuries has been the progress of the Atlantic Idea. More than anything else, this powerful political philosophy, growing out of earlier roots in Greece, Rome, Judea, and Europe of the Middle Ages and Renaissance, characterizes the modern West, whose institutions embody the Atlantic Idea. This Idea now deserves to be called Atlantic because of the prominent part America and Canada have played in its continuing development.

The issue we face today is much greater, and of much longer historical sweep, than the question of "Communism vs. Capitalism." Communism is changing, and Capitalism has changed almost beyond recognition; the power balance in the world (involving, for example, the rise of China) could bring about a different set of *political* and *economic* relations between what is now the Soviet bloc and the Atlantic West. But in terms of the most essential aspects of life, centering on *fundamental beliefs about Man and his relations with other men,* there is still a yawning gulf between east Europe-Russia on the one hand and west Europe-North America on the other.[2]

The boundary—which today we call the Iron Curtain—between the two traditions, the one of authoritarianism, the other of freedom, has shifted with different eras. In 1810, at the height of Napoleon's power, it was on the English Channel. In 1825, the Russian Decembrists raised a fleeting Atlantic island, then soon submerged in the Eastern Sea. In 1848, in the wake of the liberal revolutions that swept the

---

[2] The geographic unity of Europe, including, as it does in De Gaulle's concept, European Russia, is a poor guide to the separation of things that matter most from things that matter less. In one of the classical expositions of the Atlantic Idea and historical community, *The Zone of Indifference* (New York: G. P. Putman & Sons, 1952, p. 209), Robert Strauss-Hupé pointed out discerningly the vitally relevant historical fact: "Americans were not 'Westernized'; they were Western from the beginning; Russia was 'Westernized' yet did not become Western."

Continent, the boundary of the Atlantic system ran temporarily around much of Germany, with penetrations farther east, and down into Italy. In 1919, the boundary embraced Scandinavia, Switzerland, and Czechoslovakia; Germany, Italy, and Austria (as it turned out) precariously; and all the European lands west of the Rhine. By June 1940, the boundary once more was on the English Channel, facing the "Thousand Year Reich." The Iberian Peninsula, with the brief exception of 1808–1814, has lain largely outside the Atlantic system.[3]

The overriding issue between the two systems, the one now Russian-dominated, the other Atlantic and American-led, is not the organization of the economy, but the nature of Man, in the deepest sense, and his relation to the state.

It would be wrong to contend that there has been no recent trend towards liberalization in Russia. There have been important changes in elite perspectives and in the degree of dissent which has so far been tolerated. It would be equally wrong to conclude that the essentially totalitarian Russian system will move appreciably towards the West in less than a number of decades.

The assimilation of the border lands to the Atlantic system is a long-range historical process and in no case is it a foregone conclusion. Our brief glance showed how the line of demarcation has swayed backwards and forwards in the center of Europe. But the new political unity among the components of the Atlantic system appears, on balance and in long historical perspective, to be establishing—and defining—the Atlantic Idea more securely than ever before and enhancing its power of attraction. It is only this pulling power of an idea which, over the long run (and we may be dealing in 20, 50, or even 100 years), can eventually make

[3] If this quick sketch seems to throw some strange bedfellows (e.g. Hitler and Stalin, Metternich and Napoleon) together, that is precisely our intention. To understand this, one should conceive of the political spectrum not as a line, from left to right, but as a circle. If you move far enough away from Atlantic democracy to the left you meet those coming around from the right. The meeting point is tyranny.

the Iron Curtain irrelevant, bring the sometime parts of the Atlantic system back securely into the fold, and gradually incorporate new members, even Russia herself, into a peaceful, free Europe.

Only if approached in such long-range historical terms does the present situation or the long-term outlook for Europe, east or west, fit into a rational pattern.

THE RUSSIAN EMPIRE IN EUROPE

At the height of the Cold War, any criticism within the Soviet bloc could be—and was—denounced as treason. When tensions began gradually to subside, partly because Soviet policy necessarily changed following Khrushchev's disastrous Cuban adventure and partly because people on both sides of the Iron Curtain were fed up with the Cold War, a more favorable atmosphere emerged inside the Soviet bloc countries for discussing problems hitherto hidden. Although Soviet regression towards neo-Stalinism was apparent to experts by the spring of 1965, to Western publics it seemed until the Czech invasion of August 1968 that a gradual evolution, a softening of the Communist system, was coming about. Many assumed that détente was bound to bring more liberalization, and liberalization was bound to bring more détente, and eventually the Iron Curtain would be no more.

Unfortunately, things have not happened that way. On a time-scale of several decades, they may. But within the span of our generation, it seems more likely that we can look forward to successive prospects of increasing unrest in the Soviet bloc, followed by Russian repression, followed by new pressures which cannot be accommodated by the system inherited from the czars through Stalin, followed by still more unrest, followed by still more repression—and so on.

George Kennan asserted that "The Russians did not intervene in Czechoslovakia to re-establish a military balance.

They intervened out of their internal weakness."[4] Soviet tyranny relaxed somewhat after Stalin. Freer rein, always within limits, was given to the expression of criticism and to literary deviations from the Communist norm. But criticism, becoming more outspoken and audible, made the men in the Kremlin nervous. When the Czechs, in their ill-fated "Prague Spring," began wholesale to unbutton vital aspects of the Communist system (and most particularly the press), the Russians became alarmed. Walter Ulbricht appears to have sounded the tocsin most loudly: the still largely Stalinist regime in East Germany would not be able to withstand such pressures from a fellow East bloc country. And the prospect of Western-style democracy in Czechoslovakia, spreading like an epidemic to the rest of the Soviet empire, including Russia itself, was too much for the Kremlin. On August 28, 1969, a Russian military machine repressed freedom, as it had in 1849 in Hungary, in 1905 in Russia itself, in 1945 in Poland, Rumania, Hungary, and Bulgaria, in 1953 in East Germany, and in 1956 in Hungary.

The 1968 Setback

Certain realities are evident since August 1968. East European trends towards liberalization, modernization of economies, personal and press freedom, and contacts with the West—towards "Atlanticization," (for that is what it is)— have all been set back. The USSR is still prepared to use crushing force in dealing with its satellites, to impose strict limits on dissent, no matter what the cost. The chances for such countries as Czechoslovakia to slip out of the Russian fold are more remote than ever, if indeed they ever really existed after 1945.

Although Western trade with the East may continue to increase, and more talks with the Russians about nuclear arms control may go on—and even lead to limited agreements—real accommodation between the two halves of

[4] *International Herald Tribune,* Paris, September 23, 1968.

Europe appears further away than it was four or five years ago.[5]

THE SEARCH FOR DÉTENTE

France, Britain, Italy, the United States, and lately West Germany have all taken a hand at trying to "promote détente" with the Soviet Union and parts of her empire. The smaller Western countries, particularly in the realm of commerce, have also had a hand. In 1967 the NATO Allies agreed, in adopting the Harmel Report, to try to pursue détente as a collective exercise. They had only just begun when Czechoslovakia erupted. But they have since reiterated their determination to lessen tensions, with the aim of an eventual "peaceful settlement in Europe," albeit accompanying this declaration with one of equal determination to fortify NATO's defenses.

Even allowing for backsliding in 1968, tensions between the two blocs have lessened since the Cuban crisis in 1962. Contacts of all kinds have increased. Neither side thinks so much of the other in black and white terms (although the Russians have shown how easy it is to resume a hard propaganda line), and there have been limited but successful agreements designed to forestall a nuclear holocaust.

The record of efforts to promote détente is impressive, beginning with the conclusion of the Austrian State Treaty in 1955. The USSR became party to a treaty on the international status of the Antarctic, to the Nuclear Test Ban Treaty, to the Outer Space Treaty, and to the Nuclear Non-Proliferation Treaty. Various Western countries have concluded commercial airline agreements with the USSR, the "Hot Line" was installed between the Kremlin and the White House, and the U. S. relaxed its position on East-West trade. The Soviet Union and the United States have agreed

[5] A European, Max Kohnstamm, recently put the issue this way: "no compromise is possible between the attitude of someone who says, 'I know the truth; I alone have the whole truth,' and the attitude of a man who says, 'I do not know the full truth—we must together move towards the truth, find truth'" (in *The Atlantic Community and Eastern Europe: Perspective and Policy*, note 1, p. 98.).

to increase the number of their consulates in the other country and have relaxed restrictions on tourists. An astronaut rescue agreement was recently concluded. Cultural traffic between East and West has by agreement been considerably increased in the last decade. Tacitly, the Russians have conformed to various Western agreements, such as fishing rules off the Grand Banks.

By these measures to encourage détente, however, the United States and its allies have also stimulated a public willingness to believe that the Russians are more peace-loving than they actually are. The girdle of the Cold War has become uncomfortable over the years; there is a powerful public urge not just to loosen it, but to take it off entirely.

THE CONTROL OF NUCLEAR WEAPONRY
AS AN ATLANTIC PROBLEM

Worldwide agreements on measures to lessen the likelihood of nuclear armageddon are of vital importance to every country, without exception. Most of the agreements which the U. S. and USSR have taken to control strategic weapons, however, suffer from a serious weakness: some important countries, particularly China and France, have been unwilling to take part. If such arms control agreements cannot be truly worldwide, at least as a starter including all countries with potential capacity to make nuclear weapons in the foreseeable future, then the essential purpose has not been adequately met.

It is hard not to argue, however, that resolute attempts must nevertheless continue in the hope that the number of parties can be increased and the control measures improved as time goes on. The issue for mankind was well put recently by Max Kohnstamm, Vice Chairman of the Action Committee for the United States of Europe:

This situation [the fact of nuclear capabilities] confronts us with a staggering task: to create something completely new, unknown in history, namely, lasting peace. Whatever may be our disagreements, this situation must lead us all to one common conclusion:

that in these circumstances any policy worth the name must be a utopian policy—that is, a policy striving to establish a state of the world that never existed before. Any policy that is not, in this sense, utopian, accepts nuclear destruction, now or later. Our only choice is between different utopian policies, different utopian models, or resigning ourselves to nuclear destruction one day.[6]

The recently-signed Non-Proliferation Treaty illustrates the difficulty of achieving big-power agreement on utopia. Two years of tough negotiating accomplished a good deal, but the Treaty's weaknesses are evident. Each party, for example, has the right to withdraw from the agreement on three months' notice if it were to decide that "extraordinary events, related to the subject matter of this Treaty, have jeopardized the supreme interests of its country." Non-nuclear parties to the Treaty will face no more than the pressures of diplomacy and international public opinion if they deem it sufficiently in their interest to "go nuclear."

An early provision of the draft Treaty was dropped from the final version at insistence of the Soviet Union: the explicit right of a combination of western European or NATO powers to develop a common deterrent under supranational control. It has been asserted by the United States that because the signed version of the Treaty is silent on the subject, it does not preclude eventual creation of a European nuclear force.[7]

This sort of question poses a dilemma which is likely to recur: Can the Western countries afford to make global agreements which impair their own capacity to continue their political coalescence, or to defend themselves collectively?

The Atlantic premise, that the coherence of the Atlantic system is the *sine qua non* of the preservation of our civiliza-

[6] In *The Atlantic Community and Eastern Europe; Perspectives and Policy*, note 1, p. 99.
[7] Secretary of State Dean Rusk told the Senate Foreign Relations Committee that the Treaty would permit only the nuclear force of a federated Europe that inherited the successor rights of constituent nuclear powers—France and the U. K. (*Bulletin*, Department of State, Vol. LIX, No. 1518, July 29, 1968, p. 133.)

tion, argues that where global agreements on nuclear weaponry would be achieved only at the expense of Atlantic unity, then the preservation of unity should take precedence. This is not, however, to suggest that unity in the West and global agreements on nuclear weaponry are antithetical. In the majority of cases, such agreements help to reinforce unity if negotiated with full consultation.

NATO's military strength, the political resolve of the Atlantic system which stands behind it, and the commitment of U. S. strategic power have for more than two decades constituted the main instrument for keeping the nuclear peace of the world. Nothing on the horizon suggests that the validity of this concept will soon change.

There is no apparent way to insure that there will never be nuclear war (or war with other equally terrible weapons, some perhaps yet undiscovered) unless all powers with these arms establish an international authority to which they give up all such weapons and the means of producing them, as first proposed in the so-called Baruch Plan.[8]

Until the day, undoubtedly far off, when such a worldwide agreement is concluded, the nearest approach would be to create such a multinational authority among those powers which are able to accept the necessary controls. Hence the serious proposals for a common European or NATO nuclear arm.[9]

Meanwhile, it is clearly wise to continue to work with Russia and any other powers which are willing to consider lesser means at least to reduce the hazards. Agreements like the NPT or the Test Ban Treaty, or such SALT agreements as may be reached, even if imperfect, help to point the way to better agreements at a later stage.

[8] This plan for international control and ownership of all atomic power, including weapons, was proposed by U. S. representative to the UN in 1946, and vetoed by the Soviet Union then and again later in 1948 and 1949.

[9] One of the most creative but little-noticed proposals along these lines was made in 1963 by the then Dean of the Yale Law School (later Under Secretary of State) Eugene V. Rostow. He argued for establishment of an Atlantic Atomic Energy authority very much along the lines of the Baruch Plan. ("A New Start for the Alliance," *The Reporter*, April 25, 1963, pp. 23–29.)

There are powerful inducements for both the U. S. and USSR to come to a further meeting of minds in this field. A state of "sufficiency" in central weapons on both sides appears to have been reached. The basis for hope exists that the Russians must realize that they will never be able to pull ahead of the United States decisively; and hence they may now feel that rough parity is worth settling for. The United States, pressed severely to trim its defense budgets, has equally persuasive reasons to agree on a workable arms moratorium.

Although there will continue to be grave limitations on arms control agreements imposed by the continued unwillingness of the USSR to allow adequate on-site inspections, new technologies may in the future, as they have in the past, render agreements more enforceable. The outlook in the 70's appears to be for partially successful, if difficult, conventions between the USSR and the West to limit certain areas of weaponry.

NATO is the obvious mechanism for coordinating the West's position with respect to global talks on nuclear weaponry. The United States will necessarily have to take the lead in most negotiations, but this lead must be accompanied by the sort of consultation instituted effectively in NATO, though at a late stage, in negotiating the Non-Proliferation Treaty.

The genuineness of a Soviet desire for real accommodation and the possibilities of reaching agreements have often been seriously overestimated by the vast majority of the public in the Atlantic countries and by a number of their leaders.

There is no greater test of diplomatic and political skill—and public sophistication—than for democracies to stay tough and strong and yet parley effectively. How to know when to parley and when not to?

The Value of Agreements

Détente means a lessening of tension only; it does not mean agreement or accommodation. The Nuclear Non-Proliferation Treaty (NPT), and the modest but hopeful measures that went before it, were not "détente"; they were "simply the dictate of an obvious and bitter situation, presenting danger for both (sides)."[10] Advanced strategic weapons technology is becoming excruciatingly expensive; each important breakthrough represents a new threat to a precarious balance and a new arms race. It is also essential that neither the U. S. nor the USSR, if they can help it, allow the other to "press the button" and incinerate the world as a result of misinterpreting the other's words or actions. Therefore, the effort to reach vital but limited agreements on nuclear weaponry would seem to be in the clear interest of both sides. But the public should not mistake such efforts for a long-lasting relaxation of tensions.

Nor should the Europeans, in particular, mistake limited East-West agreements on nuclear weaponry for signs of progress towards a general European settlement. These are two different things. Accords such as NPT come about because the U. S. and the USSR recognize a strong, mutual interest in sheer survival. This has nothing to do with increasing tolerance or respect by one system for the other. On the contrary, there is no evidence that the Soviet Union would consider any settlement on Europe which the West could conceivably accept as preferable, from her point of view, to the status quo. There will probably be no real accommodation until either Russia undergoes internal changes so that she does not regard a successful, united Atlantic system as a mortal danger, or the Atlantic system disintegrates sufficiently so that Russia can be sure of an accommodation on her terms.

To recognize this unpalatable reality is not to rule out continued effort for limited détente, for making life a little

[10] George Kennan, Note 4.

more livable for people on the other side of the Iron Curtain, for gradually working out better economic relations and encouraging exchanges of people, tourism, and so on. But if by these means the West consciously hopes that it can promote the liberalization of the Eastern regimes and the consequent break-up of the Russian empire, then its governments and peoples will inevitably be disappointed, except in the most long-range terms.

The West Germans showed dismay when their "bridge-building" policy towards eastern Europe "failed" in the wake of the Czech invasion of 1968. The policy had represented a genuine attempt to calm east European fears of Germany and to some extent it did have success, particularly in Czechoslovakia. It is encouraging that Chancellor Brandt has resumed the German effort with the understanding of his NATO allies.

THE U. S., THE USSR, AND A EUROPEAN SETTLEMENT

Europeans by and large think that U. S. participation in the affairs of Europe is indispensable, even if it sometimes affronts their dignity. Europeans also believe that the participation of the USSR, however unwanted, is inevitable. Neither America nor Russia is likely to abandon Europe, for neither could be certain that its departure would not mean the extension of the power of the other—no matter what formal guarantees were provided. If there is a settlement in Europe without the participation of the United States, it could be only on Russian terms.

As the USSR is the only equal of the United States in terms of power, it is tempting for the U. S. to deal with her alone. But America does this at her peril; it can too easily seem to be serving U. S. interests at European expense, even if that is not her intention. The United States must take the lead in meaningful negotiations on nuclear weaponry agreements or on any other worldwide matter the focus of which is the U. S.-USSR nexus, but it is essential to do so only in the closest working partnership with her European Allies.

At some point, it might be tempting for the United States to try to disengage from Europe by making a bilateral general European settlement with the USSR which involved, among other things, a "neutral," reunited Germany. There is no way to do this without thrusting Europe back into the maelstrom of dog-eat-dog balance-of-power politics and nationalism, the inevitable consequence of "neutralization" for such a strong, dynamic, and geographically central power as Germany. A settlement of this kind would probably lose Germany to the Atlantic system. The most likely solution—indeed probably the only solution—for the "German problem" is patience and the inevitable pulling power, in the long run, of a prosperous, free, progressively uniting West, which includes West Germany.

Efforts to preserve and enhance the unity and strength of the Atlantic system should thus be given priority over efforts at agreement with the Russians, wherever there must clearly be a choice.

Efforts to reach agreements about Europe's future, or about mutual troop reductions with the East, should be made by the NATO Allies collectively. This is no more an American responsibility than it is that of the west European powers. It is a joint responsibility.

NATO'S ROLE IN A EUROPEAN SETTLEMENT

NATO is much more than a defense ministry for the Atlantic system; it is a political organization, as is envisaged by the 1956 report of the three "Wise Men" and the more recent Harmel Report.

Even though several Allied powers might have to conduct actual negotiations with the USSR, NATO can serve as their common planning and intelligence center, the place to work out joint positions in advance. A role of this kind will strengthen NATO greatly and contribute to more lasting agreements. This is exactly the role NATO is undertaking.

It would also seem very much a NATO responsibility to fashion a series of contingency plans for various developments in East-West relations. A good start was made in the late 50's and early 60's in contingency plans for Berlin. The difficulties in such projections were illustrated by the Berlin Wall and later by the invasion of Czechoslovakia,[11] for both of which there was no agreed plan of response.

One field in which each Western nation has generally conducted its own separate negotiations with the Soviet Union and the satellites is that of cultural exchanges. Such exchanges may, over a long period, contribute to liberalization; there is evidence of this for Yugoslavia. But it would be hard to demonstrate clear results in exchanges with most of the other east European countries and Russia. Experience suggests this is an area where various patterns and relative advantages and disadvantages might well be studied jointly by the Atlantic powers.

ECONOMIC RELATIONS WITH THE EAST

East-West trade has been a serious bone of contention among the Atlantic Allies, who disagree on the purpose of their trading relations with eastern Europe. The United States is the principal proponent of the view that trade with the Communist countries should be under restraint as far as strategic products and longer term credits are concerned, as these add resources for possible hostile use. American business has held back from such trade as a matter of choice.

Most of the European Allies have favored conducting trade with the East largely on a commercial basis, with a view that in the long run trade might contribute to a genuine détente.

Both the United States and Europe have gradually been

---

[11] For a more detailed and very readable discussion of these questions see the book by Timothy W. Stanley, *"Detente Diplomacy: United States and European Security in the 1970's,* published for The Atlantic Council of the United States, 1970, by the University Press of Cambridge, Mass.

expanding their trade relations with the Soviet and its satellites, though the total amount of such trade is still a small percentage of total trade.[12] The whole question is now sufficiently in flux to justify joint efforts to explore Western policies for the future.

Would it be to the West's advantage to try to enter into cooperative economic arrangements with the East, along the lines of the work of OEEC in its early days? Multilateral negotiations to reduce quantitative restrictons on trade, for example, might be pursued by reviving the more or less moribund Economic Commission for Europe of the UN (ECE) with headquarters in Geneva, to which both East and West belong.

The east European counterpart of the OECD is the COMECON; the two might participate as organizations in the work of the ECE, or they might by-pass ECE and try to work together on programs of "economic détente." Whatever successes were achieved, even though minimal, might be laying the groundwork for an eventual pattern of such economic value that Russia would find it more attractive than economic warfare with cold war motives. But that is indeed a long range consideration, and a gamble.

It may be wise to reiterate a basic premise of our approach to East-West relations, namely, that the West can do relatively little on its own initiative alone to further genuine détente, still less to promote real accommodation and a peaceful settlement in Europe. The necessary changes in attitude must come largely from the other side. The West is in a strong position if it shows a genuine desire for peace and understanding whenever the other side is ready for it, but remains unwilling to give up unity or compromise principles for a spurious agreement.

[12] West German trade with the East in 1966 was valued at more than $2 billion; that of the U. K. at $1 billion; that of the United States at $375 million.

CHINA

About one-fourth of all the world's human beings today live in mainland China. China possesses thermonuclear weapons and within a few years should be able to deliver them to western Europe or North America. China has become increasingly unstable under Mao Tse-tung, who will give way to new leadership in the 1970's. Although the complexities of ruling such a vast, turbulent land appear so far to have prevented China's energies from being focused effectively on the world outside, one must not discount the possibility, indeed the likelihood, that China, perhaps within the next decade, could be the most serious menace to world peace. It is not at all impossible that Mao's successors would seek to forge national unity out of discontent by sounding the call to arms against outside "foes."

While it is beyond the scope of this book to probe seriously such a murky aspect of the future, one cannot overlook the existence of a huge, potentially powerful, alien and hostile China which may become at some point in the 1970's a new strategic argument for the unity of the Atlantic system. The development of China is also likely to condition in many ways the West's relations with the USSR and the other Communist countries. Growing Russian fear of China is evident; this in turn is conditioning Soviet conduct in Europe. Certainly the USSR has been moved to take some steps towards détente with the West in order to protect its eastern flanks. It is impossible to predict, however, how Russian-Chinese relations will develop. One should not forget the Molotov-Ribbentrop Pact of 1939.

Because China lies so far outside the NATO Treaty area, there has thus far been little disposition to include sinology among NATO's preoccupations. If there is one thing that Europeans today agree on, "it is that China is America's and Russia's headache, not Europe's."[13] Europe's sense of de-

[13] Jacques Freymond, *The European Free Trade Association and the Crisis of European Integration* (*Atlantic Community Quarterly*, Summer 1968, p. 252).

tachment poses a major obstacle to a European-American foreign policy partnership. But the necessity to avoid another Vietnam, which must rate high on both American and European agendas, suggests that quiet, continuing sharing of information about China and China policy and frequent consultations on the subject may form an increasingly important part of NATO's "foreign affairs." And the question of China constitutes yet another argument for involving Japan more intimately in Atlantic counsels.

SUMMING UP

The question of Communism versus Capitalism, while important, is not the supreme issue of our time. The yawning gulf is that between the Atlantic civic culture, in which free men govern themselves under law, and Soviet-style civic culture, in which man is subordinate to the State.

Eastern Europe and even the USSR itself are historically part of Western civilization, but (with the exception of Czechoslovakia) they have never developed a modern Western civic culture. The Czech repression shows that there will be no real liberalization in eastern Europe until the Russians either liberalize themselves or are unable to prevent others from doing so.

The West must be prepared for repeated cycles of unrest and repression in the Soviet bloc over a period of years. Despite the political weakening which this might imply for the USSR, one should not make assumptions based on Western models as to the imminence of a breakdown. In the long run only the pulling power of a cohesive, consolidated, enduring, prosperous Atlantic system, together with evolution in the East, can make the Iron Curtain irrelevant. One can think of this movement only on a very long time scale.

Meanwhile, the main business of the West is the strengthening of the Atlantic system. Some gradual progress may be expected in reducing the chances of nuclear war, but true accommodation with the Soviet Union can only come about as a *consequence* of the strengthening of the Atlantic system, not as an *alternative* to it.

CHAPTER 9

The Defense of the Atlantic System

The new helicopter ship *Moskva* passed through the Bosphorus last week accompanied by two escorts.[1]

The Times, London

THE CONTINUING THREAT

The Mediterranean and the Middle East

For the first time the USSR has large aircraft carriers under construction. The Red Navy now possesses a submarine fleet which can bring Europe or the United States under nuclear fire,[2] and this fleet is steadily gaining in strength. There is increasing evidence that Russia is developing naval power to rival that of the United States. Thus she will have capacity to support political intervention in places formerly far out of range of Soviet power. As Britain moves out of the Indian Ocean and the Far East, Russia may be expected to try to move in.

Soviet incursion into the Mediterranean Sea has begun.

[1] September 24, 1968.
[2] The Red Navy's submarines were estimated to have between 130 and 200 nuclear ballistic missiles, compared with the USA's approximately 650 submersible Polaris missiles. (*The Military Balance, 1969–1970*, London: The Institute for Strategic Studies, 1969 pp. 2 and 8.)

Allied estimates of Russian naval strength there have included the *Moskva*, with guided missiles and thirty helicopters, ten or more submarines plus depot ships, a dozen destroyers, a cruiser, a score of auxiliaries, intelligence vessels, and three landing ships. During the 1967 Mideast War, these landing ships, with amphibious troops aboard, cruised just off the scenes of fighting. The Soviet fleet puts in regularly at Alexandria, Port Said, Algiers, and Latakia. There are reports that Mers-el-Kebir, a large, up-to-date naval base in Algeria used by France until 1967, may be turned over to the Russian Navy.[3] Russian manning of Egyptian air defenses, begun in 1970, is disquieting.

So far the greatest effect of this Soviet buildup has been psychological, but this growing intrusion into the Mediterranean has potential strategic importance for the following reasons:

1. Italy, Greece, and Turkey, NATO's three most southern members, depend heavily on seaborne supplies; more than nine-tenths of the total quantity of goods carried into and out of these countries is transported over Mediterranean sea lanes.

2. The communication lines through the Mediterranean to the Red Sea and farther east (if the Suez Canal is reopened) are of considerable importance to western Europe.

3. The West relies heavily on Middle Eastern oil for its energy requirements.

4. The Russians, even in Czarist times, have always lacked —and wanted—warm-water ports.

5. Only the presence of the U. S. Sixth Fleet and other NATO forces maintains the military balance.

Speaking at the Karlovy-Vary Conference in April 1967, Leonid Brezhnev, Secretary General of the Soviet Communist Party, was reported in the press as saying there was no justification for the permanent presence of the United States

---

[3] For recent articles on Soviet strength in the Mediterranean, see *Atlas*, July 1968; *Interplay*, March 1968; and Curt Gasteyger, "Moscow and the Mediterranean," *Foreign Affairs*, July 1968.

Navy in the waters washing the shores of Southern Europe, . . . and that the time had come to demand the complete withdrawal of the U. S. Sixth Fleet from the Mediterranean.[4]

The Soviets have been cultivating the Middle East patiently since the mid-50's, sowing turbulence by arming the Arab countries, while the United States has had limited success in restraining Israeli reactions. All of this spells potential dangers for NATO and its member countries as they look forward in the 1970's. The bursting into flame of the smoldering embers in this strategic region could give the Soviets the opportunity to extend further their influence or control.

The Changed Military Outlook in Europe

NATO's central European front, after several years of relative quiescence, suddenly came alive ominously with the Warsaw Pact invasion of Czechoslovakia in 1968. The resulting change in the military balance has been much debated. The Russians and four allied armies put an estimated 650,-000 troops initially into Czechoslovakia almost overnight. A Russian army of something like 100,000 men was left more or less permanently in the country.[5] In preparation for the Czech move, the Russians called up a reported half million reservists. The speed and smoothness of mobilization, the stealth of preparation, the lightning, well-synchronized descent on Czechoslovakia all impressed NATO planners.

Warsaw Pact forces may have been weakened as a result of the Czech intervenion; could one, for example, for some years to come, expect the Czech Army to fight alongside its Communit allies with effectiveness? Also, to some degree, the blatant discrepancy between what they had been told of "counterrevolutionary plots" and forces, and the obvious unity and bitterness of the Czech people must have been apparent to the invading East Germans, Poles, Hungarians,

[4] The NATO letter, February, 1968, p. 9.
[5] Other Russian allies, East Germany, Poland, and Hungary, have had permanent Soviet garrisons since 1945. Reports have varied on the numbers of Russian and other troops used in the Czech invasion. The figures cited were reported by *The New York Times* (September 10 and October 22, 1968), attributing them to Czech military authorities.

Bulgarians, and apparently some Russians as well. But as major parts of the satellite armies had never been considered reliable "in the crunch" by Western observers, any change in their attitude after Czechoslovakia may not be significant. The USSR must rely primarily on its own troops, although the satellite armies still represent a significant military factor which must be taken into account by NATO.

What *did* change certainly in NATO estimation, as a result of the Czech invasion, was: (1) the capacity of the Soviet forces to mask the mobilization and movement of very large forces; and (2) a new deployment of Russian armies on NATO's central front, changing at least the tactical balance. Even more important, NATO planners had to make a new, more pessimistic assessment of Soviet intentions as well as capabilities, to allow for renewed instability in the Kremlin leadership. Perhaps to divert attention from Czechoslovakia (who knows?), the Russians soon after their attack began to direct the most vicious propaganda in years against West Germany. Visa requirements for West Germans entering East Germany were reinstituted. Threats were resumed against West Berlin. The Russian government declared its right, as an occupying power, to intervene anywhere in West Germany (not only West Berlin) if it thought that "undemocratic forces" posed a threat.

After several years of increasingly moderate Soviet behavior towards western Europe, these startling events were a grim reminder that the Russian ship of state, ever under control of leadership which can change its intentions or its identity overnight, can veer sharply off a given course at any time.

The sudden about face to encourage the "Ostpolitik" of the Brandt government in the fall of 1969 is evidence of the instability of Russian leadership.

AN APPRAISAL OF NATO'S MILITARY STRENGTH

Taken together, the history of the Cold War since 1946 plus the formidable Russian intrusion into the Mediterranean and the Middle East, plus the evidence since the Czech invasion of unpredictability in the Kremlin mean that the Soviet threat is still very much alive. NATO will still be needed in the 1970's and as far ahead as can now be seen.

One might think of NATO's military role in terms of "four D's": its prime job is *deterrence*; if this fails, it must be prepared to mount a *defense* and the ability to make that defense is an essential part of the deterrent to assure peace. If deterrence works, it leads eventually to *détente*; if détente grows strong enough, it could ultimately bring controlled *disarmament*. The objective is always to maintain and insure peace.

NATO's ability to deter successfully depends first on its armed strength. How good is NATO militarily?

The Sword and the Shield

NATO's power is of two sorts: first, there are the nuclear striking forces ready to inflict unacceptable losses on an attacker. This has been called the sword, prepared to leap instantly from the scabbard. The major part of this force consists of the American missiles based on land and in the sea, together with bomber squadrons. But in addition there are substantial nuclear forces in Europe under joint command of the United States and its allies, and under their joint veto power. This is appropriately known as the two-key system.

The important facts about the nuclear strength of NATO countries is that it is powerful enough to inflict fearful and unacceptable damage on an aggressor even after incurring an initial attack, and the nuclear forces are ready to act within minutes. The United States is clearly committed to their use, if needed, to defend all members of the alliance. These forces are more powerful than the forces in the Soviet Union, and there is every intention of keeping them so, or, to use the more popular language, at a level that is wholly sufficient for deterrence.

The second kind of NATO power has often been called

the shield because of its defensive nature. The review just given of Russia's use of force in Czechoslovakia showed once more that the forms aggressive Soviet action may take are varied and unpredictable. To be ready to meet such moves, the NATO alliance needs to have something more than the threat of massive retaliation. It has been clear for many years that what is required is the capacity for a "flexible and balanced range of appropriate responses, conventional and nuclear, to all levels of aggression or threats of aggression."[6]

Armed Strength in Europe

It is difficult to ascertain the true comparative strengths of the NATO and Warsaw Pact forces in Central Europe. In 1967 a staff report of the U. S. Senate Subcommittee on National Security and International Operations characterized the balance in this way:

Soviet front-line forces in central Europe are approximately matched by NATO's front-line forces in West Germany, but the Soviet Union has superior conventional forces in reserve. Furthermore, the Soviet Union typically has done more than the Atlantic allies—and sooner—to provide its armies with the most modern equipment. It is also a very weighty advantage that the main strength of the Warsaw Pact is provided by one army with uniform equipment, a centrally controlled supply system, great room for maneuver, and a single military doctrine.[7]

While the overall numerical strength on either side does not appear since to have changed substantially, the quality and deployment have been altered. For more than a decade, Supreme Headquarters Allied Powers Europe has maintained that NATO requires a minimum of thirty divisions on the Central Front; there are actually twenty-four. These face twenty Russian divisions in East Germany, five in Czechoslovakia, and satellite forces ranging in quantity and quality from six East German divisions to the uncertain Czech for-

---

[6] Communique of the North Atlantic Council, December 14, 1967.
[7] Henry M. Jackson (ed.), *The Atlantic Alliance: Jackson Subcommittee Hearings and Findings* (New York: Frederick A. Praeger), 1967, p. 31.

ces.[8] NATO divisions are generally larger than Warsaw Pact divisions.

The number of divisions does not tell the whole story. Many of the NATO units, at least prior to the Czech crisis, were not up to strength, nor had all been adequately trained. Since that crisis there has been some reinforcement, but according to NATO estimates in the summer of 1970, the quality and equipment of Warsaw Pact conventional forces have improved more than proportionally.

NATO's Supreme European Headquarters (SHAPE) several years ago recommended a minimum conscription term of eighteen months, yet several European NATO countries have cut terms to fifteen months, even twelve in some cases. Several rely heavily on volunteers but have difficulty recruiting enough. The United States has from time to time drawn upon its divisions in Europe to provide specialized, experienced personnel for Vietnam. A few combat units are prepared for prompt return to Europe by air. The United States Congress has shown restiveness over maintaining strength in Europe which European members of the alliance now have the material means, as well as the personnel, to supply, as will he discussed later.

The most serious NATO weakness arises from the absence of France from its order of battle. Missing French real estate reduces the depth of defense arrangements and brings closer the possible need to use nuclear power. The French withdrawal from its commitment to the NATO military organization leaves uncertainty among other things as to flights over French territory—now granted on an annual basis. NATO lines of communication and supply across France are effectively cut off.

In view of the recent change of administration in France, one should be clear as to the French position. France has not withdrawn from the North Atlantic Treaty, as she could

---

[8] Figures from *The Military Balance, 1969–1970*, note 2. Some NATO countries such as the U. S. and the U. K. have large numbers of their forces for national use; "NATO-assigned" forces therefore only represent part of the full strength which could theoretically be available in event of a major conflict. But the Central Front's assigned twenty-four divisions are the only ones actually "on the spot."

have done under the terms of the Treaty, on one year's notice. She still accepts the obligations of the Treaty for joint defense, and other members of the Alliance retain their obligation for the defense of France. But she has withdrawn from the integrated military organization. Her two divisions still in Germany are on an ambiguous basis; they are not under NATO command, nor are they *committed* to come under that command in time of crisis, as are other NATO-earmarked troops. The French divisions cannot be counted on, though there is a presumption that they would cooperate in any emergency.

It should be added that there is considerable informal cooperation with French officers. A French representative sits with the military Committee; there is a French mission at SHAPE; and there are many other contacts. Also the French participate in and pay their share of the NATO ground environment radar system for keeping informed on air activity over Europe. It is to be hoped that the present French Government will support and strengthen this sort of cooperation.

It should also be noted that France participates in almost all other NATO activities outside of the military, including political consultation.

The encouraging feature of this situation has been the way in which the fourteen other NATO allies closed ranks and cooperated in the construction of new headquarters in Belgium (when NATO was invited to leave France) and in carrying forward the common military program.

This episode has had one further dramatic and important aspect. It has shown the fallacy of the old idea that NATO had to be limited to action on which there was complete unanimity. The Fourteen have carried through this whole operation without France. Thus they have proved that one recalcitrant member cannot veto what a majority of the other members wants to do.

One reason for entertaining hope of greater French participation arises from a careful and professional poll of French public opinion in the spring of 1969, before De

Gaulle's retirement, on the critical question of whether France should continue its membership in the Alliance. 74.3 per cent said yes; only 11.5 per cent favored withdrawal; 14.2 per cent voted "do not know."[9] The French people seem more convinced of the worth of NATO than their government had been. A renewal of a closer association of France with the NATO command structure would help to restore the military balance in Europe.

How Integration Has Worked

NATO's deterrent power depends not only on the numbers and quality of divisions available, but on the capacity to plan effectively for their use and to command and control them. In NATO's infancy it was decided that a certain amount of "integration" of national forces under international command would be essential. Developments in the technology of war dictate the continuance of this trend. If NATO continues to be regarded as essential to the security of its members, pressures to increase the amount of integration can be expected to become even greater in the 1970's.

NATO's integrated international command structure, particularly SHAPE, has worked eminently well; high morale and excellent working relations among planners and commanders constitute an amazing achievement, considering the differences in national allegiance, customs, training, and language. Also, the willingness of the NATO countries to raise and maintain substantial (and integrated) forces over two peacetime decades is a remarkable accomplishment. However, every Atlantic country with the exception of Germany still has its own General Staff, alongside the hierarchy of NATO commands. Each has its own Defense Ministry. The pattern of command integration in NATO is only partial.

The common "infrastructure" of NATO airfields, pipelines, and communications systems—all instantly ready in event of war—is a major cooperative achievement and an important factor in NATO's deterrent power.

[9] Poll by Cofremca, Paris, April 15–May 15, 1969.

NATO's air defense system, also highly integrated, is a formidable part of the deterrent. No other air system would make much sense in an age when modern jets can streak past four or five small European countries in half an hour.

A Mobile Force has in recent years been developed to give SHAPE several battalions of powerfully but lightly armed infantry from several countries, with small tanks, artillery, and other weapons, all transportable by air in case of imminent or actual hostilities. The utility of such integrated forces is obvious, but military commanders believe that NATO ought to have its mobile capability greatly increased.

There has been little progress in standardizing NATO arms and equipment, beyond the pioneer work of the 50's. In Germany, where the bulk of NATO's ground forces are concentrated, there are still six—not one—individual logistical systems. In contrast, the armies of the four Warsaw Pact countries which invaded Czechoslovakia in the summer of 1968 all had interchangeable arms, spare parts, and everything that goes with them.

To sum up: the process of integrating the various national forces into one cohesive NATO defense system, which had proceeded well from 1950 to 1963, has been substantially halted. It would add to NATO strength if integration could be resumed and intensified.

THE NUCLEAR DILEMMA

A basic problem of another sort troubles the Alliance: the planning, management, and control of the nuclear deterrent, the backbone of NATO's defense. The crux of the problem is that this deterrent at present consists so overwhelmingly of the American strategic force, under U. S. control, plus a much smaller British strategic force, and a considerable force of short range weapons under joint control (involving a two-way veto on their use). At various times, the other NATO partners have been worried lest the U. S. would not use its nuclear forces in time—or perhaps at all—

to forestall a determined Soviet conventional attack on western Europe; or that, conversely, the Americans might, by
using their nuclear weapons, perhaps in a far-off place such
as Vietnam, engulf the Europeans against their will in a
general war.

With respect to the first fear, a good deal has been done
through a series of steps designed to give all the members
of the Alliance a greater measure of participation in nuclear
strategy. As a result of the Summit Conference of heads of
governments in December 1957, the program of setting up
NATO atomic stockpiles in Europe was decided upon, and
specific agreements implementing the plan were made between the United States and other member countries. Thus
tactical atomic weapons were made available under joint
control—the "two key" system.

In addition, steady progress was made in bringing all the
Allies into the planning operation, first by a military group
in SHAPE headquarters in Europe, then by an Allied committee based at SAC headquarters in Omaha, and, finally,
through setting up in 1966 the NATO Nuclear Defense
Affairs Committee and the Nuclear Planning Group to bring
the Europeans into the planning and management of the
British and American nuclear deterrents.

Over and beyond these specific steps, the pressing forward of political consultation within the Alliance gave
greater assurance that all might share in the understanding
of basic factors involved in the prior events which might
conceivably lead to the use of nuclear power.

To some extent, these steps have convinced the Europeans that the issue of "whose finger on the trigger" is not
so important as they had thought, so long as they are kept
fully knowledgeable about American nuclear developments
and have a chance to participate in contingency planning
and are consulted on underlying basic problems.

The issue, however, is by no means dead, as was illustrated
by the difficulties encountered in negotiating the Nuclear
Non-Proliferation Treaty in 1967 and 1968. The French,
who developed their own independent nuclear force com-

pletely apart from NATO, refused to participate in drafting the Treaty, let alone sign it. The German Government long delayed signing, partly because they feared that the Treaty would interfere with peaceful commercial uses of nuclear power and partly because some feared it might foreclose the possibility for either an independent European nuclear force—which some day might be a logical adjunct to a European political and defense union—or an integrated NATO force.[10]

In the last analysis the German Government was far-sighted enough to recognize the necessity for preventing the spread of this dreadful engine of destruction and to see the political hazards of seeking for itself nuclear capability.

This unresolved nuclear dilemma has had unfortunate effects on NATO's strategic planning. The strategic deterrent forces on which NATO depends are trained, planned for, and commanded quite outside its control. It is true that American strategic planning must cover the world; NATO's planning is confined to Europe and its approaches. It is not surprising therefore that, in practice, much of NATO's strategic planning actually starts out as U. S. planning, sometimes presented to America's partners as *faits accomplis*.

The search has however been going on for further means of giving European states wider participation in some form of nuclear deterrent. One attempt in this direction was the American proposal of 1960–61 for a Multilateral Force (MLF), an ingenious plan for jointly owned and controlled vessels carrying nuclear weapons. After long and painful discussions, the plan was quietly interred in 1965 when it became apparent that neither Congress nor the European Allies would back the idea nor be prepared to spend the money it required. For a time the British Government espoused a variant, the "Allied Nuclear Force." The Europeans have been ambivalent and contradictory in their

---

[10] The United States signed the Treaty, according to Secretary Rusk's testimony before the Senate Committee on Foreign Relations, with the tacit understanding that it would not foreclose the creation of such supranational forces. But the condition he placed on such a force—*i.e.*, its subordination to a federal authority—would be difficult to meet. (See page 150.)

attitudes towards acquisition of nuclear weapons, whether jointly or separately. The British and French examples are not encouraging in terms of costs and results.

The United States, after lengthy and sober consideration, seems determined to retain control over use of the awesome weapons, insofar as possible. American legislation is strict on this point, and the anti-proliferation treaty further embodies this decision in international law.

In the last analysis this nuclear issue is insoluble without instituting what in effect would be a true federal government covering most of the Atlantic countries, at least in the spheres of defense, foreign policy, and much economics. The trend in this direction, although in a long-range sense it may be said to exist, is slow and uncertain indeed. In the meantime the United States has regarded its control over nuclear weapons as in effect a trusteeship for world peace, and the Allied governments have been more prepared to entrust this final, terrible authority to the President of the United States than to anyone else.

SHARING THE BURDEN OF NATO

Under present conditions NATO overall troop strength in Europe can hardly be cut with safety. The situation could change if there were progress towards a more genuine détente with the USSR, as described in Chapter 8, or if the quality of NATO forces were improved by such measures as attracting more volunteers, lengthening service terms, providing better weapons, and achieving more effective integration in training, logistics, and command.

But what is most important is this: if cuts are to take place, they should be made (1) pursuant to a joint NATO decision, after the most careful consideration, and not as unilateral *faits accomplis* by members; and (2) if possible along with comparable Warsaw Pact reductions.

Cuts or not, is the common NATO defense burden being shared fairly?

Military expenditures as percentages of gross national

product and as absolute figures are shown in the following
table:

DEFENSE EXPENDITURES[11] OF NATO COUNTRIES[12] IN U.S.
DOLLARS FOR 1968 AND 1969, AND AS PERCENTAGES OF
GROSS NATIONAL PRODUCT FOR 1968.

Country	Defense Expenditures 1968–69 (US $ million)		Defense Expenditures as percentage of GNP
	1968	1969	1968
Belgium	501	519	2.4
Britain	5,450	5,438	5.3
Canada	1,589	1,678	2.5
Denmark	292	336	2.3
France*	6,104	5,586	5.3
Germany**	5,900	6,050	4.5
Greece	318	382	4.3
Italy	1,940	1,930	2.7
Luxembourg	7	8	1.0
Netherlands	898	940	3.9
Norway	320	344	3.8
Portugal	302	321	6.2
Turkey	472	510	3.9
United States	79,576	78,475	9.2
Total NATO	103,669	102,517	

* Includes some items of the military nuclear program not shown in the
budget of the Defence Ministry. The 1969 Figure is calculated at the post
August 1969 devaluation rate of exchange.
** Includes financial assistance to West Berlin.

[11]Source: The Institute for Strategic Studies, *The Military Balance 1969–1970*,
London, 1969, p. 57
[12] Excepting Iceland, which has no defense expenditures per se.

It should be noted that these figures are for total military spending, not just amounts spent for NATO. For the United States they are worldwide, including Vietnam. For most European countries their expenditures are largely chargeable to NATO, with England and Portugal as partial exceptions.

U. S. defense dollars buy less than many others because of high pay and fringe benefits and more plush practices.

Also it should be noted that Germany offsets part of the costs of U. S. forces in Germany by buying U. S. military hardware and in other ways.

Even bearing these facts in mind, it is clear that the U.S. is carrying a disproportionate share of the cost of defending Europe. Europe is indeed the frontline point of contact with its Soviet bloc, but its own people should assume a larger share of their own defense. American expenditures are a serious drain on the balance of payments which has been heavily in deficit for several years, while a number of European countries, especially Germany, have had large surpluses.

It is not surprising therefore that a body of opinion in the United States—and particularly in the U. S. Senate—favors withdrawal of the bulk of the U. S. forces now in Europe. The invasion of Czechoslovakia gave this effort pause, but on January 24, 1970, Senator Mansfield introduced a resolution into the Senate, the opening paragraph of which was as follows:

It is the sense of the Senate, that with changes and improvements in the techniques of modern warfare and because of the vast increase in capacity of the United States to wage war and to move military forces and equipment by air, a substantial reduction of United States forces permanently stationed in Europe can be made without adversely affecting either our resolve or ability to meet our commitment under the North Atlantic Treaty . . .

By deciding in the summer of 1969 to cut its forces in NATO by roughly half, Canada gave encouragement to this sentiment.

Those who favor withdrawal argue that American forces were placed in Europe on the understanding that it was a temporary measure to bridge the postwar period in which the European Allies were regaining their economic strength. Recovery has taken place, yet European defense contributions are not proportionate to American.

Several things may be said in reply:

First, because of the French withdrawal, NATO needs U.S. forces more, not less, than before.

Second, under U. S. leadership NATO formally adopted a strategy of "flexible response" in 1967. This commits the Alliance to strong conventional as well as nuclear forces to contain accidental or experimental hostilities (the kind most likely to occur on the long NATO European front) and to hold back attack from the East long enough to clarify intentions on both sides without resorting to nuclear weapons. NATO's aim, to be able to make an appropriate reply to enemy aggression at any level, requires strong conventional forces of considerable versatility. A weakening of the power for such response would bring closer the risk of resorting to the use of nuclear arms.

Third, when the United States reduces its force commitments to NATO, the Europeans tend under present conditions to reduce, not increase, theirs. In an inflationary prosperity, with unstable political leadership in many countries, Europeans discount the danger of attack from the East, and argue that the only real defense is nuclear and that therefore their own efforts could make little difference militarily.

Fourth, if NATO reduces forces without a Russian *quid pro quo*, the chances of negotiating a reduction in Soviet bloc forces are lessened.

Fifth, the presence of strong U. S. forces contributes to the maintenance of political stability in Europe, east and west.

The security afforded west Europeans by the presence of U. S. troops is still a vital factor in the diminution of old conflicts and rivalries, in the confidence of political regimes, and in their ability to withstand Soviet diplomatic pressures.[13] NATO's forces so far have not stopped the Russians from aggressive suppression of popular uprisings in East Germany (1953) and Hungary (1956) or from the throttling of liberalism in Czechoslovakia in 1968, but if strong armies had not stood on the Western side of the Iron Curtain at these times, the upheavals could have erupted into western Europe. As a result of the Soviet invasion of Czechoslovakia, it is more important than ever that the West Germans feel certain that the United States would resist any crossing of their fronters by Russian or satellite forces, now much closer to Bavaria than before.

Sixth, if U. S. forces were pulled out of Europe, only to be sent back in event of war, they might not be able to return in time or in sufficient force because of the speed of a probable attack and the disruption of the theater of war, of landing fields, etc.

Finally, it is well to remember that American troops constitute a pledge to Europe, including the nuclear commitment. Their very presence is a guarantee of American intervention if and when needed. They are thus an essential part of the deterrent against another world war.

In short, U. S. troops will be needed in Europe well into the 1970's, perhaps longer. The numbers can be reduced safely only in consultation and by agreement with the NATO Allies on an effective strategy of defense.

Despite the handicaps, it should however be possible for the Europeans, gradually, to assume a larger share of the burden. This will depend in part on the evolution of the political framework of relations with the Soviet and the evo-

---

[13] Without NATO—and particularly the American support for NATO—the West Germans could hardly have withstood the intense pressures on West Berlin. At one time or another, Norway, Denmark, France, Italy, Greece, Turkey, and Great Britain have all been targets for Russian intimidation.

lution of the Atlantic system, as will be discussed in later chapters of this book.

NATO'S DEFENSE PERIMETER

The Treaty was quite specific about the territory it covered:

any of the Parties in Europe or North America . . . Turkey or . . . the islands under the jurisdiction of any of the Parties in the North Atlantic area north of the Tropic of Cancer; . . . forces, vessels, or aircraft of any of the Parties, when in or over these territories or any other area in Europe in which occupation forces of any of the Parties were stationed on the date when the Treaty entered into force on the Mediterranean Sea or the North Atlantic area north of the Tropic of Cancer.[14]

If a Russian naval attack were made on Pearl Harbor, the NATO Treaty as it now stands would require no response by the fourteen Allies. Both Alaska and Hawaii were territories in 1949; both have since become States. Alaska was originally covered by the NATO Treaty; Hawaii was not, and still is not, a curious anomaly.

More potentially serious is the question of NATO's attitude were there an invasion of a European nation neither a member of the Warsaw Pact nor of NATO. This was spotlighted following the Czech invasion, when the Yugoslavs feared that the USSR might attack them, too, to extirpate, root and branch, the budding plant of liberalism.

Strategically, any Soviet move towards occupation of Yugoslavia would be of great importance. A glance at the map suggests why: Soviet submarine bases and airfields on the Aegean could directly menace Italy. The strategic positions of Greece and Turkey would also be endangered. The pressures on Austria, surrounded on three sides by Soviet forces, would be intensified. Thus a Soviet threat to Yugoslavia would be a threat to the West's position in central Europe,

[14] Article 6, The North Atlantic Treaty.

the Mediterranean, and the Middle East.

Not long after the Czech invasion, the press contained references to Austria too: "Polish Premier Josef Cyrankiewicz hinted ominously at the danger of West German influences in Austria ... "[15] As signatories of the 1955 Treaty by which Austria was unburdened of occupying armies, Britain, France, Russia, and the United States did not undertake any specific guarantees of Austrian integrity or neutrality. But subsequently the Austrian Parliament passed a law declaring its perpetual neutrality. It is conceivable that the USSR, with a new crisis in a satellite, might feel constrained to "reoccupy" Austria on some pretext associated with its postwar "rights."

Finland, although by its own efforts still independent, could again be menaced. There was speculation in October 1968[16] that the Russians might call for military consultations under the Finnish-USSR Treaty of 1948, as they had in 1961, with a view to securing their Finnish flank in the face of alleged pressure in the Baltic from the Germans and Scandinavian members of NATO.

NATO should consider soberly and in depth the implications of any such eventualities, which might not necessarily take the form of direct military attack, but of political pressure. These are considerations reinforcing the need to keep NATO strong, mobile, and alert.

OUTSIDE THE NATO AREA

What has been said earlier about developments in the Middle East and adverse European reactions to American policies in Vietnam make it clear that the future of NATO depends a great deal on what any of its members does outside of specific NATO boundaries. Lack of cohesion of the members of the Alliance on such matters weakens morale and the strength of the NATO ties. But more than that,

[15] *International Herald Tribune*, Paris, September 28-29, 1968.
[16] *The Times*, London, October 10, 1968.

world peace hangs in the balance when NATO mem-
ers face world Communism outside, as well as inside,
Europe.

Every inquiry into NATO policies, and specifically the
1956 report of the three "Wise Men" and the Harmel report,
agree on this.

NATO should not forget that the influence and interests of its
members are not confined to the area covered by the Treaty, and
that common interest of the Atlantic Community can be seriously
affected by developments outside the Treaty area.[17]
The North Atlantic Treaty area cannot be treated in isolation from
the rest of the world. Crises and conflicts arising outside the area
may impair its security either directly or by affecting the global
balance.[18]

Also the methods of dealing with this problem are agreed
upon and have been tested, but are inadequately practiced.
They are, in brief: mutual information; mutual thorough consultation, as far in advance of actions as possible; and the
utmost effort to reach agreed policies in NATO, the UN,
OECD, and other international organizations.

Perhaps more than any other NATO task, the ability to
find a core of cohesion on these difficult questions will constitute the test of whether or not NATO can measure up to
its great opportunities.

NATO'S POLITICAL STRUCTURE

Almost every important question in NATO has encountered
head-on the uncomfortable fact of European fragmentation
and relative weakness *vis-à-vis* the United States. If the
United States carries a disproportionate share of the burdens
and makes most of the important decisions resentment can

---

[17] Report of the Committee of Three quoted in NATO Facts and Figures, NATO
Information Service, Brussels, 1969, p. 307.
[18] Harmel Report on the Future Tasks of the Alliance, *Atlantic Community Quarterly*, Spring 1968, p. 117.

develop and initiative, resolve, and self-sacrifice among the others suffer.

To get around this problem of the "giant and the pygmies," a number of structural changes have been suggested.

1. *A European grouping within NATO.* This might range from informal consultations to separate staff and organization for defense procurement and production, or even to the equivalent of a European Defense Ministry or Community. The latter suggestions imply a higher political authority to cover a number of purposes, going beyond what even six European countries have been able to achieve thus far in the European Economic Community.

   The nearest approach to such a grouping for defense has been the Western European Union, which has certain specific powers of administering the terms of the arms limitations agreements with Germany. They have considered and made resolutions on some more general military questions, but they have never spoken in NATO as one voice. European and United States military questions are so intertwined that a separate European grouping has never seemed to make much sense.

   The question of whether such a European Defense Community would have nuclear armament or not is a key question. A Europe united for defense and economic matters would speak with a great deal of authority; it would speak with even greater weight if it possessed nuclear forces. The United States would then want to think long and hard about assisting the creation of such a deterrent, as it has assisted British nuclear weaponry. To warrant such a step the EDC countries would have to satisfy essential security requirements and also agree on a single locus for the necessary political and administrative powers—*i.e.*, the authority to pull the nuclear trigger. Europe is still a long way from satisfying these requirements, nor indeed has there been any substantial evidence of desire to move in this direction.

2. Another alternative would be to create a *North Atlantic Defense Community*, similar to the EDC just described but including the United States and probably Canada. This would mean replacing NATO with a sort of half-way house between its present stage and a federal defense union, a giant step, especially for the United States. But if the defense of the Atlantic system is indeed indivisible, if this indivisibility is not simply a product of the Cold War, as we have suggested, but rather a fact of history which will hold true for as far into the future as we can see, and if there are now difficulties because NATO itself lacks adequate power to serve the common interest, then the idea of a North Atlantic Defense Community is worthy of serious consideration.

A North Atlantic rather than a European Defense Community better fits the security indivisibility of the whole North Atlantic area.

Such a far-reaching proposal would not, by itself, correct the imbalance between Europe and America, but it would help. Because it would provide a more effective instrumentality, the Europeans might respond to such a bold venture rather than to continue relying on persuasion, with limited results. As of now they would participate in an organization where each nation has a vote of its own, but they would feel that each vote had greater weight.[19]

3. Another less ambitious proposal for changing the balance of power in NATO has been to appoint a European

---

[19] If the United States desired a much tighter form of defense union on Atlantic scale or with some combination of European and Atlantic supranationalism, and this involved more sharing of nuclear power, it would be necessary to amend the McMahon Act (the Atomic Energy Act of 1946 and 1954 as amended), a most formidable roadblock to any arrangement for sharing nuclear weaponry. Such sharing has so far taken place only with the United Kingdom.

as Supreme Allied Commander of Europe (SACEUR). Two difficulties always arise when this is discussed. One is the possession of the final nuclear power by the United States and the close relation between SACEUR and the U. S. President. There is also the problem among Europeans in agreeing on a SACEUR from among themselves. It may well be that a European personality will appear of such stature as to overcome both these difficulties.

A return of France to more active military participation in NATO would help in maintaining a better balance between Europe and America, in terms of size of forces and skilled leadership.

Pending such changes, it would be wrong to overlook the very real European influence in NATO under the present organizational structure. Europe has provided four Secretaries General: Ismay, Spaak, Stikker, and Brosio—all men of great ability and influence. Other European leaders, both civilian and military, have helped materially in NATO achievements. The opportunity for such leadership is wide open for the future without a major change in structure.

CONCLUSIONS

While it remains for later chapters to develop further some of the questions raised here, it may be helpful to attempt to strike a kind of trial balance on the future outlook for NATO.

First, there is no escaping the conclusion that, under present conditions, NATO remains essential to the security of western Europe and America. A balance of military power, both nuclear and conventional, must be maintained in relation to both the Soviet Union and Communist China. There must be no misunderstanding of the capability and will of the West to meet any aggression with such a response as would clearly be unacceptable to the aggressor.

Equally, it must be clear that the NATO Allies are prepared to discuss and negotiate agreements upon methods of limiting and reducing expenditures on arms. Their objective is peace, and they arm only as a deterrent and defense against war and aggression. New scientific discoveries have made possible new methods of surveillance of arms control with less difficulty than heretofore, and thus are reducing one of the obstacles to agreement on the control of strategic weaponry.

The central problem of NATO is to maintain a balance between military power and progress towards effective peace-keeping arrangement. One of the greatest dangers lies in letting hope outrun reality and yielding to a false sense of détente. With democracies, in which the people's will dominates, maintaining this balance is not, and will not, be easy. It will need wisdom and the most inspiring leadership that can be summoned to the task.

The NATO record is remarkable. To preserve an Alliance with its breadth of principle and its steady strength for these twenty years has been a great achievement. The real test, however, is not yesterday's accomplishments but the answers to today's demands. These call for re-examination of structure, of personnel, and of the will of the governments which make up NATO. Future success cannot be assumed.

Second only to the danger of a false détente, NATO's greatest weakness arises from a lack of cohesion on major world problems outside the immediate NATO area. United States policies on Vietnam, right or wrong, have been divisive. The only corrective thus far suggested is a thoroughgoing increase in consultation on such questions, in advance of final decisions whenever this is possible. The objective should be to reach generally agreed positions.

Underlying many NATO problems has been an inherent weakness in structure due to the predominant position and power of the United States. No fully effective means has thus far been devised for correcting this imbalance which arises from the very nature of the Alliance and its present military and economic composition.

Over the years a number of steps have been taken to give European members of the Alliance greater participation in the planning and arrangements for nuclear weapons. The fearful character of these weapons has convinced the United States and most other countries of the need for limiting control over them as closely as possible, and this principle has been reflected in the Non-Proliferation Treaty.

The most promising structural alternative to the NATO Alliance would appear to be a much more binding federation or defense community. This would involve further sacrifice by the participants of limited elements of sovereignty. Thus far this step has not yet commended itself either to the European countries as a group or to the Atlantic countries as a whole. Even this would not by itself entirely correct the dominant influence of the United States.

We have suggested above a number of changes within the present framework which would give NATO better balance. The return of France to some form of participation would help greatly. A willingness on the part of the European members to contribute a larger share of the military forces and the costs would entitle them to a larger share of the commands and a stronger voice in the counsels.

Finally, NATO like most other human institutions, reflects the character and capacity of the people who run it. This means the permanent representatives of governments who compose the North Atlantic Council, the members of the staff, the military commanders high and low, and back of them the people in the member governments who work on broad policies and who come to meetings of the Council. NATO has been fortunate in these people, particularly in the Secretaries General and the military commanders, and the support they have received from the member governments. The officers who have served successively on the

NATO staffs, and others who have attended the NATO Defense College, constitute a corps of loyal friends whose support is invaluable. This is, more than anything else, the key to NATO's future—the dedicated, able people ready and willing to keep it the world's greatest power for peace.[20]

[20]The role of leadership in the building of all Atlantic institutions and the methods which might be employed in a deliberate effort to select, train, and inspire leaders was discussed in an article by James R. Huntley in *Orbis,* published by the Foreign Policy Research Institute, University of Pennsylvania, Spring 1966, page 106ff.

CHAPTER 10

NATO as a Political Instrument

The Alliance affords an effective forum and clearing house for the exchange of information and views; thus each ally can decide its policy in the light of close knowledge of the problems and objectives of the others.[1]

The Harmel Report

In a rudimentary way, NATO has been laying the groundwork for an "Atlantic foreign policy." By 1955, the essential military structures and forces were in place. The North Atlantic Council began to turn its attention increasingly to the common diplomatic problems of the members. Until that time, guidelines for joint dealings with the USSR on Europe's future had been largely settled by the Allied "Big Three," as occupying powers of Western Germany and Wartime partners of Russia. But with the creation of a German Federal government and its accession to NATO, it became fitting to discuss in NATO questions of arms control, European security, and—as time went on—the global range of the Communist threat.

In 1956, the NATO "Wise Men," in presenting their report on steps which the Alliance could take to further col-

[1] Harmel Committee, December 1967, reprinted in the *Atlantic Community Quarterly*, Spring, 1968, p. 145.

laboration in non-military spheres, laid greatest stress on deepening and broadening "political consultation." In 1967, after a decade disturbed by French military withdrawal, a committee under the Belgian Minister of Foreign Affairs, Pierre Harmel, came up with recommendations reinforcing those of 1956 and urging that NATO become specifically a forum for concerting Allied efforts to reach a peaceful accommodation in Europe with the USSR.

NATO's political achievements in developing a "coalition foreign policy" and settling disputes among its members, while limited, are noteworthy. However, these accomplishments are less obvious or spectacular than the dramatic successes in building a common defense against Soviet military encroachment in Europe.

This is partly because non-military action has had less publicity. What is done, for example, in political discussions cannot be thrown open to the public without destroying the prospect of success. Furthermore, dangers averted seldom reach news columns.

But there is a still deeper reason: in the non-military field, the NATO members are trying to harmonize political policies, some of which may affect their deep-seated national interests. François Duchene explains the problem well:

Overall policies are, by definition, the very language of free will and can only be made fully common when sovereignty itself is jointly and not separately exercised. It follows that the areas of divergency between allies must first be reduced by intermediate forms of cooperation if the chances of common political action are to be enhanced.[2]

It would be too much to expect complete harmony of view among the members of NATO, or of the U.S. Congress, or of any other free body, but NATO action can and often does bring governmental policies closer together.

To understand this operation, it is necessary to clarify in

---

[2] François Duchene, *Beyond Alliance* (Paris: The Atlantic Institute), 1965. p. 35.

our minds the sort of mechanism and organization which NATO has at its command for non-military operations, and then to review the kind of action which may be expected. A clarification of this sort is basic to an appraisal of the likelihood of future progress and to any consideration of changes which might be made to improve the result.

THE NATO MECHANISM

NATO represents an entirely new kind of diplomacy. The core of its mechanism is a select group of representatives of member countries who have their offices in the same building, who meet together regularly as the North Atlantic Council, and who confer privately as well. These representatives are not simply mouthpieces of their governments, as they are sometimes pictured. Each ambassador is responsible for two-way communication between NATO and his own government as well as interpreting to his associates in NATO his government's policy, which he often helps to form.

In most cases the ambassadors represent several departments of their governments. The United States Ambassador, for example, is the Representative at NATO of the State Department, the Defense Department, and to a degree the Treasury Department. Under the Eisenhower Administration he had the right, when in Washington, to attend the meetings of the Cabinet and the National Security Council, and had direct access to the President.

The daily association of these fifteen Ambassadors is a novel form of diplomacy which has proved to be of great value.

The second important element in the NATO organization is the staff of international civil servants headed by the Secretary General. Each one of the four Secretaries General who has served NATO had earlier been a cabinet member in his own country and a man of international distinction. He and his deputies occupy a position which has been, and can be, of great influence.

Still a third arm in the NATO mechanism collects and presents facts and statistics. As in two or three other international organizations, the process is a new method called "confrontation," in which each member country submits to an annual review of its military and economic position before the North Atlantic Council. This review, now modified to a "Five Year Rolling Plan," attempts to measure in facts and figures what each member country is doing in relation to its share of the NATO program. High government representatives from each country under scrutiny, in addition to its Permanent Representative in NATO, participate in these reviews.

There are additional links between NATO and the member governments. These include a joint meeting of Foreign Ministers at least twice a year, one of which the Finance and Defense Ministers also attend. There are frequently other meetings for specific purposes attended by specially qualified people from the member countries. In December 1957, partly in response to the Soviet launching of Sputnik, the heads of government met as the North Atlantic Council.

A further link between NATO and its members is provided by the North Atlantic Assembly (formerly the NATO Parliamentarians' Conference). This group, comprising legislators from the fifteen countries, has since 1955 held annual sessions of five or six days' duration to discuss the problems of the Alliance and to adopt resolutions and recommendations addressed to the NATO Council and governments. Although the Assembly has no official status, its budget is covered by the national parliaments and its annual sessions, usually held at NATO headquarters, are attended by key NATO and government officials and the press. The Assembly is briefed by the Secretary General and by SACEUR and addresses its recommendations to the NATO Council and governments.

The Assembly has had great value in keeping an influential group of members of parliaments interested in and informed about NATO affairs. Through its debates, it has helped to bring matters of NATO-wide interest before the publics, and has frequently made useful suggestions. There has been a wide range of proposals by the Assembly itself and others for converting the organization into an official consultative body with greater influence. In 1969, the North Atlantic Council took the unusual step, for the first time, of replying formally and in writing to recommendations and resolutions of the Assembly. From such humble beginnings grew the power of many national parliaments.

POSSIBLE KINDS OF POLITICAL ACTION

We come now to the key question: What kinds of action may be expected from the NATO organization? Lord Ismay, the first Secretary General of NATO, wrote of

the NATO method—*i.e.*, the technique whereby the representatives of sovereign governments reach unanimous agreement without formal vote.[3]

This unique way of describing NATO's work recognizes that action is taken without necessarily complete unanimity, for under this formula every member does not have to vote, or even register formal abstention, but a workable consensus is nevertheless achieved.

In most descriptions of NATO action, this important innovation in political technique has been overlooked. For example, in *NATO-Facts About The North Atlantic Treaty Organization*, published in January 1962 by NATO's own Information Service, the statement is made:

the North Atlantic Treaty Organization has no supranational character; all decisions are taken unanimously by national representatives.

[3] Baron Hastings Lionel Ismay, *NATO, The First Five Years*, Paris, 1954, p. 48.

The description goes on to say that this does not imply the right of veto, although the language is ambiguous.

In the light of twenty years of experience, it seems clear that both these definitions of political action in NATO are too limited. There is, in fact, a variety of actions that have been taken in or through the North Atlantic Council which do not involve a vote; the purpose of all these is to influence the policies of the member countries by contributing information, analysis, and points of view rather than to come to a formal vote on the questions concerned.

The U. S. Government has since 1950 taken the position that (1) no nation could be forced in NATO to take action against its will, but that (2) no nation could prevent joint action which others wished to take. This principle has been applied to conspicuously good effect since French withdrawal from NATO joint defense activities in 1965. Further recognition and application of this concept would enhance NATO's effectiveness.

One might clarify as follows the kinds of action that NATO can take:

1. *Decisions by Unanimity*: The only requirement for unanimity specified by the Treaty concerns the admission of new members. In practice, however, additional questions have generally been decided by unanimous vote. These include the appointment of Secretaries General and Supreme Commanders, and the apportionment of financial contributions; in other words, major administrative or financial questions. There have been some cases, however, involving the financing of major infrastructure projects in which only the countries primarily concerned have reached agreement among themselves and proceeded without the agreement of others.

2. *Action by Consensus*: This may be illustrated by discussions in the North Atlantic Council of arms control proposals which Western countries intend to submit in meetings with the USSR. These proposals have as a mat-

ter of course been discussed in advance by the Council, with a free expression of opinion by all members. A consensus of views is reached by discussion, without necessitating a vote or complete unanimity.

The same procedure has been followed in regard to Council discussions of messages received and answered by member governments, in the long exchange of communications between the USSR and the Allied nations; views expressed by different NATO partners and by the Secretary General have always been given consideration by the countries directly involved, but no voting has been required.

Still another illustration is found in the recurring proposals for dealing with crises in Berlin, which have habitually been submitted to the Council by the member countries directly concerned, and have received a consensus of support. Somewhat the same thing happened when the Soviet Union deployed missiles in Cuba in 1962; the other members of the Alliance supported the countermeasures taken by the United States, as they had supported the position of the United States during the U2 incident in May 1960.

3.   *Information and Discussion*: On many occasions various member countries have put before the NATO Council information about activities in which they were engaged, usually in advance of action, so that there might be an opportunity for discussion. This is the process which might most correctly be called "consultation." The U. S. and U. K. involvement in the Lebanon and Jordan crises of 1958 are examples.

4.   *Information*: This term applies to situations in which urgent action is required, giving little opportunity for discussion. Hence it can hardly be called consultation.

If the curtain of confidence could be lifted, a complete calendar of the discussions and actions taken by NATO, classified under these four different headings, would show a surprisingly wide range of such activity. Such political action represents hours and hours of meetings of the Council, its committees, and informal groups. Action requiring unanimous consent is thus only a small part of NATO's activities; indeed, some of the most effective harmonization of policy does not require unanimity at all.

HOW THE NATO MECHANISM CAN PRODUCE UNITY OF ACTION

To understand how these various types of discussion, although often without power of decision or command, can yet lead to harmonized Allied policy, it is necessary to analyze the process of national policy making.

In the foreign affairs ministries of democratic countries, the formulation of policy involves three successive stages: determination of the facts, recommendations as to policy or action, and decision.

Determination of the facts and their significance is essential but not always easy. Information comes from a variety of sources, including diplomatic, military, or other intelligence, other governments, the press, or business. "Facts" gathered in this way are often conflicting. Therefore an agreed assessment of the facts and their significance must be reached before action can be recommended.

Recommendations for policy and action are ordinarily initiated at a relatively low level and pass both upward and outward to obtain concurrence, or agreed modifications, by all concerned. Where there is substantial agreement on the facts, agreement on the policy or action required is usually easier.

Where there is agreement on both the facts and the recommended policy, decision presents few problems. It is only when there is substantial disagreement at lower rungs of the policy-making ladder, or need for a drastic change in existing policy, that recommendations require top-level decision.

Throughout the entire process, up to the moment of final decision, there is constant interplay between the government and its representatives in the country or countries concerned to secure agreement on the assessment of changing facts and on the right policy to be followed.

What relevance do these standard processes of fact finding, policy recommendation, and decision have for NATO?

Joint Formulation of Policy

There are no easy answers to most major issues which arise in NATO. There is often strong divergence of views between certain governments on such matters as force levels, strategic concepts, and the control and use of nuclear weapons.

Yet questions of foreign policy can, except with respect to the powers of decision, be dealt with internationally, in such a body as NATO, by much the same process as that used domestically. To some extent this is already being done.

Determination of the facts has long been done jointly by the intelligence staffs of SHAPE, SACLANT, and other NATO military commands on the basis of information received from many sources. Similarly, the NATO International Staff and the political and economic committees of the Council draw information from member governments on any situation they believe merits NATO attention. This process has been improved considerably since a new NATO Intelligence Center at Brussels came into operation in 1968. The advantages for the Alliance should be obvious: even such varied situations as Vietnam or the Dominican Republic would be far more tractable if there were substantial agreement on the facts and their significance.

NATO not only collects and assesses intelligence, but it can formulate recommendations as to policy or courses of action to be followed. Finding the right policy requires a combination of objectivity—in the search for the answer which will be best from the common rather than from one national point of view—and of political practicability in realistic understanding of varying national interests and policies.

The process of joint policy formulation has been evolving over the years in NATO, as well as in OECD and the European Communities. Good results have been obtained by task forces drawn from both the NATO International Staff and the national delegations most concerned with specific problems. Constant interchange between NATO headquarters and the various capitals has been shown to be essential. The greater the competence of all the diplomats and specialists involved, the more effective the results, and the more responsibility governments are willing to entrust to this new process.

The process can at times be facilitated by meetings of senior officials concerned with specific problems or areas in the various Foreign Offices, such as those heading regional bureaus or policy planning staffs.

Wide areas of agreement among most Allied governments can usually be reached. Experience has shown that unanimity is not essential. Governments which disagree can hamper decisions but can rarely block the policy to be followed if a majority of others concurs.

As NATO is still an intergovernmental, not a supranational, body, the power of final decision remains with national governments. That is why we must speak of common or harmonized policies permitting concerted action by the nations concerned, rather than of a single or united policy and action. Yet there is no reason why the problems of final decision cannot be reduced in numbers and importance simply by expanding gradually the areas of agreement.

Consultation outside the Treaty Area

Subjects discussed in the NATO Council over the past two decades were not by any means confined to events happening in the NATO geographical area. While Article 5 of the Treaty commits members to take appropriate action "to restore and maintain the security of the North Atlantic area," it was clear from the beginning that the security and prosperity of the members of the Alliance were also mightily affected by events and decisions outside that area. For example, there was general recognition that employment of nuclear weapons by any member of the Alliance, in any part of the world, was of concern to all members. From the point of view of Atlantic security, this is, indeed, one world.

There are, however, certain limitations on action with respect to matters outside the Treaty area, as, for example, cases in which another regional organization or the United Nations is working for a peaceful solution. While it is desirable and helpful for members of the Alliance to discuss in the North Atlantic Council the implications of such problems for all of them, the Alliance has generally refrained, for example, from taking a NATO position on a subject under current debate before the United Nations.

A similar principle, which developed out of NATO experience, is a recognition of the individual responsibility of NATO members in certain areas. For example, the United States individually, and as a member of the Organization of American States, clearly had a special responsibility as to Cuba, which the other members of the Alliance respected. This has not, however, prevented Cuba from being discussed by the North Atlantic Council frequently in an effort —not always successful—to reach a consensus on wider aspects of the situation there.

ASSESSING NATO AS A POLITICAL INSTRUMENT

A former high official of the U. S. Government once asserted privately that the United States, ahead of all the other NATO governments, explained to its allies early and confidentially its policies and plans for all parts of the globe. While this is true, explanation is only part of an effective system of consultation. To make the Atlantic system work smoothly, its member countries must be willing not only to explain their policies and plans, but to bring to their allies the chief international problems and issues *before* they reach the stage of decision. Allied suggestions, no matter how constructive, can have little effect once the great wheels in Washington, for example, have ground out a policy.

There was little effective consultation in NATO before the Kennedy Administration decided to increase drastically the number of American military advisers in Vietnam, or immediately after the Tonkin Gulf incident. "The United States involved itself in Vietnam all alone and without authority or even consultation with the North Atlantic Alliance."[4]

The Vietnam War is now becoming history. But more Vietnam-like problems may arise, and the United States will again have to make crucial decisions. If it wants the Atlantic Alliance to extend its influence beyond the prescribed NATO area, or even to retain the confidence of its allies, it will have to take its allies into its confidence at the earliest possible stages of such important issues, listen to them and sometimes (not necessarily always) stand willing to be guided by the merits of their individual or cumulative advice. Turning the still fluid Atlantic system into something politically better requires that each member be prepared sometimes to accept the judgment of its partners even though their recommended course would be different from a decision which might be made in isolation.

The same principle applies to all Allies. The Suez affair in 1956 was, like Vietnam, damaging to the Alliance. There is no question of any Ally being compelled to do something it does not want to do. Effective consultation involves sharing the best available intelligence from any source, jointly eva-

---

[4] Thomas K. Finletter, former U.S. Ambassador to NATO during that period, in *Interim Report* (New York: W. W. Norton), 1968, p. 175. For an enlightening account of later development of the consultative process in NATO see *NATO: The Transatlantic Bargain* by Harlan Cleveland (New York: Harper and Row), 1970.

luating its significance, and considering possible courses of action from various points of view.

Unless the United States and its allies share essential intelligence, discuss issues with one another before they are fully formulated, and consult deeply before the choices between policy alternatives are made, the United States will all too often have to bear the overwhelming responsibility and burden of decisions.

If, on the other hand, the Atlantic Alliance is able to develop this procedure, beginning in the early stages of any potentially dangerous situation, the United States will reap at least two major benefits. One is better policy decisions, taken in the broad perspective of various points of view. The other is a reasonable hope for wide support for those decisions, and consequent willingness to accept a share of responsibility for carrying them out.

Experience suggests, however, that only consultation which leads to *joint policy formulation* can approach the goal of common policies and action on matters of important consequence to the Western world.

IMPROVING NATO'S POLITICAL MACHINERY

The OECD in some of its operations has provided valuable examples of how joint policy formulation—the next step beyond consultation—can work.

One national representative on OECD Working Party III (monetary affairs) made nineteen trips to Paris in two recent years to meet with colleagues from the foreign offices, treasuries, and central banks of the twenty-two OECD members. In such intimate, almost constant contact with each other and with an important problem, the dimensions of common interest and, often, the direction of common solutions are seen more readily. Such working parties can, in fact, and sometimes do, compose joint policies for adoption by the OECD governments.

NATO working parties have likewise proved especially

effective when they have included the government officials who deal day to day with a particular problem in national capitals, where final decisions have to be made. This practice could well be expanded in NATO in seeking a higher degree of harmonization of Allied foreign policies.

A study conducted in late 1968 by the private Atlantic Council of the United States for the Nixon Administration suggested several ways in which NATO's political machinery might be improved.

1. The North Atlantic Council should seek to progress from consultation to increasingly wider and more effective policy coordination and, finally, to joint policy formulation.

2. More active use should be made of NATO's new Intelligence Center, to which all Allies now contribute information on situations of common interest. Joint evaluation of intelligence in the early stages of situations can be helpful in leading to joint policy recommendations.

3. There should be a more formal, official relationship between NATO and the North Atlantic Assembly.

4. The North Atlantic Council might consider establishing a NATO advisory commission of a few distinguished citizens who would not represent governments, but would serve in their individual capacities to make recommendations reflecting the common interest on long-range matters. This might turn out to be the embryo of a body similar to the Commission of the European Communities.

5. The U. S. Ambassador on the NATO Council, remote from his capital, should spend more time in Washington involved in the U. S. policy-making chain of command. He should be assisted by a deputy who could alternate with him in Brussels and Washington.

These relatively modest steps, if taken, could have useful and important results. Similar modifications could improve OECD. But the burden of this book is that shoring up the structures which met the needs of the late 40's and 50's will not be enough for the mid-70's and beyond. In a crisis, consultation, "joint policy formulation," and a tighter organization are all helpful but often inadequate. The problems and circumstances call for a body that can take swift, firm decisions. Short of the development of a supranational structure with federal characteristics for the Atlantic community, there can be no wholly satisfactory solution to the decision-making problem. This must, as of today, be a long-range goal, but it needs our full consideration. The question will be reviewed in the next chapter.

CHAPTER 11

Towards a Larger Framework

Each man's experience starts again from the beginning.
Only institutions grow wiser; they accumulate collective experience, and owing to this experience and this wisdom,
men subject to the same rules will not see their own natures
changing, but their behavior gradually transformed.[1]

HENRI FREDERIC AMIEL

THE CASE FOR A BETTER FRAMEWORK

The thesis of this book is that a strong case exists for making
the Atlantic system more resilient, more capable, more enduring. To summarize that case:

1. The Soviet threat, the reason for NATO's creation, is
   still present and will be deterred only if the Atlantic
   nations preserve an effective common defense system.
   Nor will any long-range accommodation with the Soviets be possible without such a system. The advancing
   technology of warfare requires increasing defense integration: the question of a common political authority for
   nuclear weapons has not been solved. The fair sharing

[1] Swiss philosopher writing in his Journal a century ago.

203

of defense burdens also requires a more adequate political framework.

2. The transatlantic economy at present is outrunning the available political structures. In a few years it may prove unmanageable unless the Atlantic powers establish an orderly framework for industry, trade, and finance so that economic growth is consonant with the highest political ends and ideals of the Atlantic system.

3. The Allies have different degrees of interest in different parts of the world. Some, notably the U. S. but also others to some degree, feel responsible for carrying out major policies in these places. Others have little interest but do not hesitate to express opinions. The Allies cannot go on indefinitely pursuing conflicting, or unilateral, policies on issues of major importance in non-Atlantic parts of the world. The Alliance could hardly withstand the psychological strains of more Vietnams. We must find a way to agree on at least the main lines of approach to such central problems.

4. Western Europe enjoys peace today, but this peace rests on an uneasy equilibrium which could be upset one day unless the Atlantic system is effectively consolidated. In particular, the three great powers of France, Britain, and West Germany must be linked within an Atlantic structure by mechanisms which bind their peoples together with ties of self-interest and common objectives powerful enough to meld their national patriotisms and aspirations into a larger, harmonious, enduring equilibrium.

5. Building a world peace system and a lasting accommodation in Europe depends in large measure on the contributions of a strong Atlantic system.

6. The social, psychological, technical, educational, political, and philosophical problems of modern urban society are common to the Atlantic countries. Their chances of dealing successfully with these problems—many of them new to any society—will be better if they ap-

proach them together, sharing information, experience, ideas, and evaluations of their respective performances. As the real cement of the Atlantic system—and its fundamental purpose—lies in its common values, it is not only fitting but probably essential in the long run that our countries deal in common with the question of adapting these values to the modern setting and building on existing institutions to reflect those values.

7. Military alliance of itself is not enough. Nor is just coordination of foreign policies. Nor is economic cooperation alone. Certainly static treaties and intergovernmental conferences are not enough. What is needed is the dynamic development, at whatever pace may be practicable, of a comprehensive, growing pattern of joint effort and understanding in major fields of human endeavor.

8. Finally, only a truly great idea will inspire youth and guide its energies and idealism into channels which can make a positive difference in the state of affairs. The creation of an enduring Atlantic system is such an idea.

For all these reasons, the Atlantic peoples must now look far ahead and fix their eyes on a common goal, no longer content simply to undertake whatever common task the immediate moment dictates but resolved to make the most of their interdependence. A larger, better political framework is necessary.

THE STRAW MAN OF SOVEREIGNTY

Many people, accustomed all their lives to the pre-eminence of the nation-state, balk at the idea of wider unions because, they say, "We shall have to give up sovereignty." Like so many words, *sovereignty* is a symbol; it is a legal and political emblem of theoretical freedom of action and full power and authority externally and within one's borders.

But sovereignty is also a red herring. The United States gave up some sovereignty when it signed its first treaty in

1788. Every treaty or international agreement represents a limitation of sovereignty. The pressures of events in an interdependent world impose *de facto*, if less evident, limitations. But for almost every cession of "sovereignty," America has gained advantage for its own interests.

All the members of the United Nations, except the Big Five, who retained the right of veto, gave up a potentially major part of their sovereignty when they subscribed to its Charter. One should note that without the presence of the veto in the Charter, it is doubtful if any of the Big Five, including the United States, would have accepted it. It might be an interesting speculation to ask, with the advantage of hindsight, if the United States might be better off today had it not insisted on maintaining its "sovereignty," and accepted establishment of a vetoless UN.

The United States, along with other countries, gave up some freedom of action over its monetary affairs when it joined the International Monetary Fund—but it gained for the American people and all others a greater, more stable prosperity. Numerous arbitration treaties have helped to avoid bitterness over border adjustments and other minor matters. U. S. airlines generally accept passenger fares set by the International Air Transport Association, sometimes against their own will—and thriving international air travel has added to everyone's prosperity and convenience.

The Rio Treaty, creating the Organization of American States, and the NATO Treaty obligated the United States to go to the aid of its allies if they are attacked—but these Treaties also greatly increased the security of Americans and strengthened peace in large areas of the world.

The United States could not cope alone with the Gold Crisis of 1968 but consulted her allies and agreed on a common program of action, and—with all the others—put it into effect. This has sustained the prosperity of all, in which the American people share.

The modern world would be in a sorry mess today without such abridgment of the unqualified national freedom to act.

There are no longer independent countries—only dependent ones or interdependent ones. If we are not willing to accept as a reality our interdependence with others and make it effective through give-and-take agreements and common institutions for planning and execution, then all of us—even the most powerful—risk eventually becoming somebody's dependents or subjects.

INSTITUTIONS AS A MEANS OF BUILDING UNITY

Some students of politics claim that institutions can only be a reflection of political unity, which must exist before the institutions can be created. In testimony before the Jackson Subcommittee of the Senate, in 1966, Professor Thomas C. Schelling addressed this problem:

Ratification of the NATO Treaty did not create this obligation, the commitment or the interest; it expressed it.[2]

Carrying this argument a step further, it is obvious that institutions can be no substitute for consensus or political will. The now moribund Southeast Asia Treaty Organization, NATO's pale shadow, is a case in point.

Institution-building as a path to international community has limitations. Yet, if we accept the necessity of building effective unity for the Atlantic peoples, it is evident that institutions must play a powerful role. Uwe Kitzinger, editor of the *Journal of Common Market Studies*, puts it this way:

Now, of course, institutions are not enough; they are no substitute for policies, or for their execution. It is the policies and their execution that matter. But without the institutions, as we have seen all too often, the right policies are difficult enough to formulate and all too often quite impossible to adopt and then to execute.[3]

[2] Henry M. Jackson (ed.), *The Atlantic Alliance: Jackson Subcommittee Hearings and Findings*, (New York: Frederick A. Praeger), 1967, p. 153.
[3] *The European Common Market and Community* (London: Routledge and Kegan Paul), 1967, p. 206.

This has been the lesson of the European Community. Whenever the common political will was ripe, the institutions were ready with the programs and the means of carrying them out. And the Community's institutions have sometimes carried the Six along with a kind of built-in momentum even when political will was flagging. Much the same can be said for the United Nations, whose most encouraging progress has been in the achievements of its specialized and associated agencies.

One of the best cases for new institutions and common programs is that they are educational. By putting old problems in a new framework, one forces the parties to confront them together. This idea has probably been the central contribution of Jean Monnet, whose bold concepts and driving initiatives lay behind the creation of all three European Communities. Once set up, institutions have a way of becoming common interests in themselves, capable of carrying the members beyond their original objectives into a new sense of community and common achievement.

Until comparatively recently the nation-state was considered the ultimate political unit. Within its boundaries modern industrial units expanded into highly organized and powerful vested interests. More recently these same vested interests have burst the bounds of the nation-state. Their interests, ownership, and operations are increasingly multinational. They need, and may be expected both to demand and to pioneer, new methods and new institutions for dealing with problems which respect no frontiers.

There is no more important long-term issue for the Atlantic system than that of developing and bringing into being common political institutions that can endure. To endure, they must be practical, based naturally upon past and present experience, but adapted to the needs of today's and tomorrow's world. And they must serve the interests not of the state but of the individual.

WHICH PATH TOWARDS UNITY?

Three broad solutions have been advanced to the problem of a stronger Atlantic framework. One, the "functional" approach, holds that the pressures of the modern world will force or at least open the way for the pragmatic development of greater unity in many fields and directions and that following the path of greatest opportunity will be the surest road to unity of action.

The second, the "Atlantic Partnership" solution, assumes that Europe will first form an effective political union of its own and then develop a new, closer relationship with North America.

The third, "Atlantic Union," seeks to leapfrog both the others and proposes a common federal government for all the North Atlantic powers, to be established, its more fervent advocates hope, by a constitutional convention.

Functionalism

Whether they like it or not, few thinking people today would deny the rapidly increasing interdependence of today's world. The effect upon the individual of distant events over which he has no control is obvious on this crowded, jet-propelled, televised, computerized, nuclearized planet. It is a vastly different world from that sparsely settled, largely rural one that our ancestors and even our fathers knew, where local events had far more effect upon the individual than distant ones, and even wars affected relatively few people.

In trying to adapt to this new world, statesmen have groped, and much of the significant progress in giving institutional muscle to interdependence has been achieved by the functional method. Much of that progress has been described in this book. The GATT, the World Bank, the IMF, NATO, OECD, the multinational corporation are all examples. Each of them represented an attempt to deal in a limited and practical way with one or more specific problems.

Yet each of them required vision as well as practicality. Each represented a compromise between various interests and points of view, a compromise disappointing to those of its proponents with the longest vision and the highest hopes. Yet each instrument has worked and has shown often unsuspected ability to adapt to changing circumstances. Each case has represented a combination of vision and practicality, of idealism and realism. Had either quality been lacking, these functional groupings would not even have been started, let alone succeeded.

Proponents of the other two paths to unity seek to go much further, much faster. Their strength is in their vision, the undeniable desirability of their goals. Their weakness, and the lack of more significant progress, has been due to their inability to overcome the hard, practical problems involved along the way, or to sheer inertia of institutions and leaders.

Atlantic Partnership

European unity has been a dream for generations. It changed from a dream to practical politics in 1948 when, at a conference of the European Movement at The Hague, the Foreign Ministers of Great Britain, France, Italy, and the Benelux countries declared it the goal of their national policies. During the 1950's it received great impetus from the practical vision of men like Konrad Adenauer of Germany, Alcide deGasperi of Italy, Robert Schuman and Jean Monnet of France, Dirk Stikker of Holland, and Paul-Henri Spaak of Belgium. It caught the imagination of politicians, intellectuals, businessmen, and of youth, who burned frontier barriers in their enthusiasm.

The preponderant view for more than a decade among European publics, their governments, and the U. S. Government has been that a union of Europe should be completed before any tight transatlantic arrangement is designed. Fully united, the Europeans presumably would feel greater self-confidence; they could then bargain with the United States "as equals." A majority of American practitioners and theoreticians of European affairs have leaned toward this approach, either because they believed that it would preclude (or at least put off) the necessity for the United States to abridge its own independence in a transatlantic union, or because they believed that it was the best practical way to move towards such a union. Some influential Americans have held that a tightly-organized federal Europe would clearly serve American interests better than a loose organization dominated (or blocked) by whichever country happened to be ascendant in Europe at any given time.

President Kennedy gave this "two-pillar" conception (the U. S. being one pillar, united Europe the other) his official blessing and a new twist by calling it "Atlantic Partnership." This slogan, oversold on both sides of the Atlantic, tended to dominate transatlantic political discourse during the 1960's. Partnership was presumably to be effected once Europe had reached fairly complete union, so that it could "speak with one voice." However, in only one field so far, that of international trade, has even a part of Europe—the Common Market—reached a sufficient degree of unity to be able to bargain on a par with the United States. Europe's unification has been proceeding far too slowly for "Atlantic Partnership" to be considered an early possibility.

Could the United States agree to settle important affairs if Britain, for example, were not represented by the European federal bargaining partner?

Another obstacle to the Partnership idea has been the problem of providing a place for Canada or any western European nation unable or unwilling to join the EEC nucleus.

Still another obstacle has been the lack of assurance that the Atlantic dialogue would improve with the creation of an "equal" bargaining power in Europe. Henry Kissinger, President Nixon's chief White House foreign affairs advisor, argued persuasively in his book *The Troubled Partnership*[4]

[4] Published for the Council on Foreign Relations by McGraw-Hill (New York), 1965.

that such a development might conceivably make Atlantic disagreements worse.

If Europe were to unite, but then draw away from the United States—forming in effect a third force—the result could be to weaken the strength of the West in dealing with the East. The now quiescent but troublesome nuclear debate could again surface. The more probable danger is more of the same disunion and inaction on an Atlantic scale which has impeded the progress of the EEC in recent years.

The civic character of a "Third Force" Europe might also be in doubt. It could be a question of sheer numbers. The civil service, the European Parliament, the Europe-wide political pressure groups and voluntary associations, the legal profession, the mass media—in short, "the Establishment" of a united Europe—would probably be dominated by nationals of the three largest Continental nations, no one of which has yet made a coherent modern democracy, in the deepest sense, truly its own.

If a united Europe were to veer off on its own course tomorrow, it is unlikely that Britain—if she were a member —and the small democratic countries of Europe would be able alone to complete the process of assimilating Italy, France, and Germany to a mutually consistent Atlantic civic culture.

Lest Americans be complacent, it is entirely possible that the civic development of the United States itself will proceed more surely if it becomes even more firmly bound to the countries of northwestern Europe within a strong Atlantic system.

There is room for serious doubt that Europe, or even the six members of the Common Market, can soon become united to the same degree as the United States. The unity of the United States, in essence, is not one of states but of *people*—of the cultural heritage of all the countries of Europe, and others. The United States is in large measure a united Europe, developed over centuries of high mobility in a new and common environment.

Apart from the argument over whether or not Atlantic Partnership, if achievable, would be a good thing, the chief difficulty with the idea is that it implies postponing structural improvements to the Atlantic system until the Europeans unite. H. van B. Cleveland puts the skeptic's case as follows:

It is difficult to believe that the aim of equal partnership with the United States has the power to move Europeans to a grand act of political construction. Europeans already enjoy the security and prosperity which are the fruits of good relations with the United States, without paying the price of union.

He also asserts:

when the chips are down the Western European nations would still rather depend on the United States for their security and political continuity than on one another.[5]

But for the United States (or any of the major European powers) now to disown the whole idea of Atlantic Partnership would be to pull the props out from under a concept which is psychologically congenial to large numbers of Europeans and indeed may offer the best hope of arousing the enthusiasm needed to turn inertia into action. On the other hand, to postpone indefinitely constructive acts which could strengthen the entire Atlantic system while waiting for European action would be imprudent.

Atlantic Union

Late in the last century and early in this one various proposals for some form of Atlantic union were made by Henry Adams, Lord Bryce, Dwight Morrow, Norman Angel, and others. In 1939 Clarence K. Streit was the Geneva correspondent of the *New York Times*. Disillusioned with the ineffectual efforts of the presumably "universal" League of

[5] *The Atlantic Idea and Its European Rivals* (New York: McGraw-Hill), 1966, pp. 139, 145.

Nations to keep the peace and a firm believer in the principles of democratic federalism embodied in the U. S. Constitution, he published in that year his book *Union Now*. In it he proposed that a federal union of all the European democracies, plus the United States, Canada, Australia, and New Zealand, be established by a constitutional convention similar to that of 1787 in the United States.

His book was widely read and discussed and the idea gained many adherents on both sides of the Atlantic. He is the true father of the "Atlantic Idea" and has worked tirelessly ever since for its realization. Streit is discounted by many as a utopian dreamer, but careful analysis of his proposal raises questions as to the validity of this criticism.

His proposal was based upon five premises.

First was the conviction that the pressures of the modern world were creating greater interdependence and required new methods and institutions to assure peace and freedom. The last thirty years have brought almost universal acceptance of this basic thesis.

Second was the conviction that governments exist to serve their people, not the reverse, and that sovereignty in a democracy resides in the individual rather than in the government. This principle is unquestioned in the democratic West but its consequences in an age of interdependence are not always clearly realized.

Third was the belief that the democracies around the North Atlantic basin shared a unique nucleus of common heritage, ideals, and interests and were thus in a better position collectively to maintain peace and freedom than any "universal" grouping. Events of the past twenty years have brought wide acceptance of this premise, too.

Fourth was Streit's conviction that federal principles, as embodied in the U. S. Constitution, by which free men grant limited specific powers to a central authority to deal with problems with which none of their smaller authorities can deal effectively, provide the most effective means of combining the strength of unity with the diversity of freedom. While federalism is little understood in many countries of

Europe and many skeptics emphasize the vast difference between the situation of the thirteen colonies in 1787 and the Atlantic world of today, no American, Swiss, Canadian, Australian, or citizen of another federal democracy seriously questions the value of federal principles.

Fifth was the belief that an Atlantic federal union could best be acheived by a constitutional convention like that of Philadelphia in 1787. While Streit's first four premises have gained wide acceptance, it is this last one which many people still consider utopian. Yet Streit, driven by his conviction that only such a powerful "union of the free" can provide real security against nuclear war or monetary and economic collapse, continues to insist with urgency that time is short, and may be shorter than we think.

During the last thirty years the Atlantic Union idea has, at one time or another and in varying form and degree, obtained powerful support.

In Europe, the supporters have included Winston Churchill, Lord Avon (Anthony Eden), Robert Schuman, Konrad Adenauer, Paul-Henri Spaak, Prince Bernhard of the Netherlands, and many other respected leaders. In Canada, former Prime Minister Pearson has spoken out for it forcefully. In the United States it has been advocated more strongly in words than in action (and sometimes more strongly before taking office than after) by Presidents Eisenhower and Kennedy, Secretaries of State Dulles and Herter, and Under Secretary of State Clayton. In recent years, the idea of Atlantic Union has been publicly acclaimed by such diverse presidential contenders as Robert Kennedy, Eugene McCarthy, Barry Goldwater, William Scranton, Nelson Rockefeller, and Richard Nixon.

Of these, Nelson Rockefeller has been the strongest and most outspoken advocate. In his book *The Future of Federalism*, published in 1963,[6] he stated:

The federal idea, which our Founding Fathers applied in their historic act of political creation in the eighteenth century, can be

[6] New York: Atheneum, 1962, pp. 59-60.

applied in this twentieth century in the larger context of the world of free nations—if we will but match our forefathers in courage and vision . . .

Political creation, not improvisation, is the order of the day. And anything less than a grand design—a major idea and a lofty sense of purpose—is too puny for the time in which we live . . .

In a more recent book, Rockefeller quotes Lester B. Pearson on the need for a limited Atlantic Union:

There are, of course, many phases of the relations between NATO members, between the states of this embryonic Atlantic community, which should be conducted in the normal diplomatic way. But in the field of defense and foreign policy, those relations, as I see it, should be centralized and coordinated in a mechanism which in some respects at least would serve the same purpose— and operate in the same way—as a cabinet does in a democratic country.[7]

European Attitudes Towards Atlantic Union

The concept of Atlantic federation has much less support in Europe than that of European federation. There are a number of reasons.

One is lack of experience with federalism and understanding of its principles. Only Switzerland has had a federal union comparable in age with that of the United States. The only other European countries with federal constitutions, Austria and Germany, have had relatively brief experience with it and are actually far less federal in character than the U. S. Many Europeans thus think erroneously of federalism, particularly in connection with the United States, as implying an all-powerful central government rather than as the guarantor of local autonomy. Some might be willing to see this in Europe but few would relish it on an Atlantic scale.

[7] *Unity, Freedom and Peace* (New York: Random House), 1968, p. 146.

Another reason why Atlantic federation is not widely advocated is the head start of the "European" idea and the strong popular support it has achieved.

A third reason is the reaction, as the countries of Europe have regained prosperity and self-confidence after the material and psychological losses of World War II, against "dependence" upon the United States, which federation is thought by many to imply. This understandable human feeling gave De Gaulle's anti-American policies a wider and more subtle influence than many Europeans would care to admit.

This desire for "independence" *from* the United States, rather than interdependence *with* her, provided fertile ground for the concept of "equal partnership," whereby a united Europe would speak to the U. S. from a position of equal power, and cooperate or not as it chose. The emphasis placed by the Kennedy and Johnson Administrations on "partnership" did much to strengthen this desire.

These factors are largely psychological but behind them is a very real, major problem—that of the disproportionate size and power of the United States compared to any free country in Europe. This causes a natural fear that preponderant U. S. influence will become "hegemony"—militarily, politically, and economically. Certainly the U. S. has never consciously sought "hegemony," although some of its officials and the conduct of some American business enterprises in Europe have undoubtedly contributed to that fear.

It is neither understood nor believed in Europe that an Atlantic federation including the U. S. would in fact go far to mitigate its present preponderance and prevent its future hegemony. Solving this problem in ways which would give Europeans a greater, more responsible share than they now have in the exercise of the combined military, political, and economic strength of the Atlantic world is essential to the achievement of a healthy, effective equilibrium between North America and Europe.

In recent years, and particularly in the last five, there has been increased questioning in Europe of the wisdom and ability of U.S. leadership to cope with its foreign and domestic problems. Vietnam and racial strife have become powerful deterrents to closer unity with the U.S.

Behind all these factors, finally, is the belief widely held by the most Atlantic-minded Europeans that the U.S., and particularly its Congress, would never accept the obligations of true Atlantic federation. Yet controversial and far-reaching actions such as ratification of the Inter-American, NATO, and OECD treaties and the enactment of legislation which led to the "Kennedy Round" of drastic tariff reductions have, after careful consideration of the advantages and disadvantages to American interests, been overwhelming endorsed by the Congress. The Atlantic Union idea has also long had significant support.

Atlantic Union and the U.S. Congress

Various resolutions calling for the appointment of delegations to explore with the Allies the possibilities of more effective Atlantic unity, including federation, have been introduced regularly in Congress since first presented by Senator Estes Kefauver in 1949.

Although the Atlantic Union Resolution was long opposed by the State Department, Secretary Dulles indicated his approval provided the delegations were named by the Congress rather than by the Administration. Secretary Herter supported it and a somewhat watered-down version was passed by both Houses in 1960.

The result was the Paris Convention of 1961, with former Secretary of State Herter and former Under Secretary of State William L. Clayton as co-chairmen of the U. S. delegation. The convention adopted a "Declaration of Paris" which expressed the conviction "that our survival as free men, and the possibility of progress for all men demand the creation of a true Atlantic Community within the next decade." To implement this purpose it called upon the Governments of NATO countries "to draw up plans within two years for the creation of an Atlantic Community suitably organized to meet the political, military, and economic challenges of this era" and to this end to appoint, "within the earliest practicable period, members to a Special Governmental Commission on Atlantic Unity . . . to propose such reforms and simplifications of existing institutions, and such new institutions, as may be required."[8]

By this time, however, the Kennedy Administration was in office with its heavy emphasis on "equal partnership." The State Department, pressing for political unification of the Common Market countries and holding that any U. S. moves for greater Atlantic unity would dilute and distract efforts towards European amalgamation, steadfastly opposed appointment of such a Special Governmental Commission.

Yet throughout the 60's similar resolutions were regularly introduced in Congress. Finally, in 1968, an Atlantic Union Resolution was approved by the House Committee on Foreign Affairs, having the support of more than one hundred Representatives and some twenty Senators. Despite State Department opposition, it had the support of all five potential presidential contenders—Kennedy, McCarthy, Humphrey, Rockefeller, and Nixon. President Nixon, in a statement to the House Foreign Affairs Committee in 1966, had expressed the view:

it is fitting that the United States, the world's first truly federal government, should be a main force behind the effort to find a basis for a broad federation of free Atlantic nations. . . . It would be foolish for us to ignore the fact that science and history are even now fatefully combining to accomplish the same goal. . . . The Atlantic Union Resolution is a forward-looking proposal which acknowledges the depth and breadth of incredible change which is going on in the world around us. I urge its adoption.[9]

---

[8] "Atlantic Challenge" by Livingston Hartley, Dobbs Ferry, N. Y.: Oceana, 1965, pp. 95-96. See also *Report of the United States Citizens Commission on NATO* (Washington: U.S. Government Printing Office), 1962, pp. 9-10
[9] "The Atlantic Alliance: Institutional Developments" by Livingston Hartley, *Atlantic Community Quarterly*, Fall, 1969, p. 324.

Substantially the same resolution was introduced again on June 5, 1969 by Representative Paul Findley of Illinois, with seventy co-sponsors. Whether, and in what form, this resolution or something like it is finally adopted by the Congress remains to be seen, but this evidence shows that it is a mistake for Europeans to believe that the U. S. Congress and the American public are less willing to consider far-reaching steps than the parliaments of Europe.

Conclusions

The main political problem of the Atlantic system is to arrive at an enduring arrangement for sharing the combined power and responsibilities of the member countries, so that they can better achieve important common purposes.

We have outlined three general methods which may be followed towards achieving the purpose: the functional approach; partnership between a United Europe and North America; or an Atlantic federal union.

Each of these three paths has its advantages, and its disadvantages.

Functionalism has the strength of pragmatism, practicality, and realism. It is happening, and has achieved remarkable results as the institutions resulting from its practice have accumulated experience and the people who serve them have learned their new techniques, and as governments have become accustomed to their novel procedures.

The European unity movement has already pioneered a flexible wider-than-national framework, has broken down many age-old psychological barriers to greater unity. It has shown that progress towards political amalgamation can be practical politics, and it has aroused enthusiam and idealism among people of all ages. Yet Europe, even if united from the Atlantic to the Elbe and the North Cape to Anatolia, is too small to deal alone with many modern problems. Still more serious are these questions: whether all of Europe, or even part of it, will truly unite in the foreseeable future, or whether it will be held back by conflicting nationalisms; or whether it might become a potentially harmful Third Force. Recent developments towards the enlargement of membership of the EEC and deepening of its coordinating powers are encouraging.

The broader framework of Atlantic unity, conceived not in a geographic but in a pragmatic, psychological sense of freedom-loving peoples with a measure of common heritage, ideals, and interest, is better suited in its scope than any other combination for dealing with the problems of today and tomorrow. Adequate political support for such a step does not yet realistically exist on either side of the Atlantic. There are , especially, deeply-rooted European fears of too close unity with the American colossus, whose wisdom is not always considered as apparent as its strength.

How can we capitalize on the advantages of each method and overcome its disadvantages?

We will always need the functional approach. To progress, the work of unification must be practical. It must respond to recognized needs and must be flexible enough to provide for later response to needs as yet unseen. Yet this steady, pragmatic process can be facilitated, given coherence, and substantially accelerated if it can be clearly seen as contributing to the achievement of challenging, inspiring goals.

The desire for European unity, a powerful force, is constructive if it is directed not merely toward creating a large nation-state but rather toward developing the nucleus for progressively wider unity.

Realization of effective Atlantic unity will require better understanding everywhere of federal principles (not merely in the American setting but also in Switzerland, Canada, Germany, Australia, and other countries) and their adaptability to an intercontinental framework. It will also require more American public support, bold governmental initiatives, and the devising of means to convince Europeans and Canadians that the risk of their subordination to the colossus is much less within a common federal framework than outside it.

No matter what the ultimate model, to bring it about will

require the most astute political leadership conceivable. And the end result will probably—like the Common Market—consist of an entirely new breed of political animal.

The essential question is: "Who will bell the cat?"

The Europeans might be reluctant to follow the American lead, yet it seems clear that leadership in any critical Atlantic enterprise must, inevitably, rest with the United States. This was true in the creation of the Marshall Plan and NATO, in transforming OEEC into OECD, in initiating the Kennedy Round, and in launching other important transatlantic enterprises. By virtue of its size and power, the United States has no choice but to lead if it wishes to attain such bold long-range goals.

But leading need not mean imposing America's will. A decent, worthy political goal for the Atlantic community in the 1980's must lead away from American hegemony, must enhance self-determination for each individual citizen, and must provide a pattern in which the dominance of any individual nation, including the United States, will quietly become a memory. Exactly what path offers most chance of success is a pragmatic question that only the future can determine. The essential thing is to keep moving forward.

To achieve progress will require above all dynamic and continuing leadership by dedicated individuals who will both carry the torch themselves and pass it on to their successors. The necessity for such leadership has been well stated by John W. Gardner:

An important thing to understand about any institution or social system is that it doesn't move unless it's pushed. And what is generally needed is not a mild push but a solid jolt. If the push is not administered by vigorous and purposeful leaders, it will be administered eventually by an aroused citizenry or by a crisis.[10]

Present leadership can mount and sustain such a new impulse only if it is capable of enlisting the energies and enthu-

[10]John W. Gardner, *The Recovery of Confidence*, W. W. Norton & Co., Inc., New York, 1970, p. 93.

siasm displayed recently on college campuses of the United States and Europe. In the ranks of student activists may be found the future leaders who will bring fresh impetus to the organizations we have been discussing in this book.

To make this possibility a reality calls for new breadth and depth of education in international affairs and the West's civic traditions; so that the new leaders can add to their enthusiasm the wisdom which comes from knowledge of man's past experience. But the primary ingredient is the will for action; this can arise only from a healthy working partnership between the present and future leadership of society in every Western country, and across national borders.

Index

225